M

W

SCREENWRITING
techniques for success

SCREENWRITING
techniques for success

Jimmy Sangster

Reynolds & Hearn Ltd
London

To Tony Hinds, who's the one mainly responsible
for me becoming a writer in the first place.

Front cover: Susan Strasberg and Ronald Lewis in *Taste of Fear*
  (Hammer/Columbia, 1961)
Back cover photograph by Uwe Sommerlad

First published in 2003 by
Reynolds & Hearn Ltd
61a Priory Road
Kew Gardens
Richmond
Surrey TW9 3DH

A CIP catalogue record for this book is available from the British Library.

ISBN 1 903111 54 4

Designed by Peri Godbold.

Printed and bound in Great Britain by Biddles Ltd, Guildford, Surrey.

Contents

Foreword

One evening, an incredible 28 years ago, I had never heard of Jimmy Sangster. Perhaps that was because I had never read the credits on a Hammer motion picture. Or perhaps it was because, at that time, I was at a boring showbusiness party on the sunny side of my second martini, engaged in the usual diversion of television producers, namely bemoaning the dearth of good writers, telling exaggerated tales of their cupidity, their inability to think originally, their ignorance of structure and their absurd dialogue in which professors and porters were indistinguishable.

I recall delivering a diatribe and summing up with: "I've just taken on a show about two truck drivers, 22 one-hour episodes and I can't find a decent story consultant."

I was talking with Joel Rogosin, a writer-director-producer famed for his skill, his acerbic humour and the merciless use of the blue pencil on scripts that crossed his desk. "I've got the perfect guy for you. He's talented. He's experienced. He's smart. He's fast..."

"And who is this paragon?" I asked.

"Name's Jimmy Sangster," said Joel.

"Never heard of him."

"He's an Englishman," said Joel.

"Hire a Brit to assign and edit scripts for a show about truckers criss-crossing America? I'm desperate, but not that desperate!"

"As I've always suspected," said Joel, "you're a *schmuck*! What do you want? An American who's an expert on truckers or an Englishman who can write?"

I wanted a writer. Badly. And I knew that anyone extolled by cranky, demanding Joel had to be a saintly genius. I didn't get home until midnight, but saintly geniuses are hard to find so I didn't hesitate to awaken the indispensable agent, hear a groggy recitation of Jimmy Sangster's daunting list of credits and set up an appointment at my office at MGM.

The next afternoon, the Brit arrived. In a Bentley. Snob that I am, I knew immediately that this guy was successful enough to afford such an automobile and discriminating and tasteful enough to reject the Rolls-Royce for the understated, elegant Bentley.

Within a few minutes I had briefed him on the concept of *Movin' On*, described the two leads, Claude Akins and Frank Converse, and tested him with a ten-line idea for an episode. He didn't like it, told me so and suggested a different plot. Chalk up another one for the Brit. The man was honest. And his story, generated in those few minutes we had talked, was a hell of a lot better than mine.

"Go write it," I said. "If I like it, you'll be my story consultant."

"Do you want it good or Tuesday?" he asked.

"Tuesday," I said, certain that I would spook this self-confident, unabashed Mr Sangster.

Four days later... on Tuesday morning... the Bentley was parked on the lot when I arrived. And the Brit was parked in my office. And his script for that one-hour show was parked on my desk.

He sat in the reception area being charming, his accent beguiling my efficient, plump and man-hungry secretary. I sat in my office, reading the script. I finished it in half an hour. It required five more minutes for me to make the only changes: 'truck' for 'lorry', 'elevator' for 'lift', 'cop' for 'bobby', 'stupid' for 'daft', 'pal' for 'mate'. And that was it. It was the first time a writer had *ever* submitted a script that I could have put on the stage without a rewrite or polish.

I briefly considered sending Joel Rogosin a case of Scotch. But I decided that validating his judgment was more meaningful for him and less expensive for me. So, I signed Jimmy Sangster as story consultant and began an odyssey and a friendship I've treasured for nearly three decades.

Within four weeks of our first meeting, Jimmy had interviewed perhaps 65 writers, all of whom had an agent, belonged to the Writer's Guild and boasted numerous credits. Not one of them came up with a coherent story idea. So Jimmy and I quickly wrote 20 story concepts; and he began making a few assignments.

Meanwhile, we had planned the beginning of our itinerary for our travelling show and assigned scripts that would be shot in a Virginia coal mine; the streets of Baltimore and the ferry on the Chesapeake Bay; at the Kennedy Centre in Washington DC; the harbour and environs of Norfolk, Virginia; then on to North Carolina and the marines at Camp Lejeune, tobacco warehouses and a cigarette factory in Durham and the stock car races in Charlotte. Although Jimmy had no idea what these places looked like, he had an instinct for developing action that utilised the location, an unerring sense of how to promote conflict between characters and, through his early experience as an assistant director and production manager, an amazing ability to protect the budget by improvisation.

Those qualities proved to be a decisive element in the success of *Movin' On*, because circumstances forced me to fire the line producer who was in charge on the road. Since it was all but impossible to find a competent replacement willing to remain on locations across the country for seven months, I had no choice but to leave the comfort of family and studio and travel with the 70-man crew. That would have been impossible without Jimmy. He became my knowledgable, respected *alter ego* at MGM.

On his own he assigned and rewrote new scripts. In time, to avoid the pain of doing all the work and giving the pay and the credit to another writer, he started writing the remainder of the scripts himself while still finding time to moderate the battles between the crusty, veteran post-production supervisor and the temperamental genius who was the musical director, as well as sending me notes on the dailies he watched each morning. On top of all that, he still found time to fly out every few weeks to join the company in Georgia or Alabama or Louisiana, and write new scenes to take advantage of spectacular settings. He was irreplaceable.

With the passing years we have worked together on television movies, pilots, and episodic series, sometimes as co-writers, often with him as producer and me as executive producer. Once, when he was shooting a musical in Las Vegas for me, he fired his production manager. Then he called me in Los Angeles to tell me, " Don't worry. I've hired a new one."

"Fine," I said. "Who is he?"

"It's you. So get on the next plane and report for work in the morning!"

Three hours later I was in Las Vegas working as producer Sangster's production manager.

And that's typical of our relationship all these years. It has been creatively satisfying and financially rewarding – although I still don't drive a Bentley! It has also been great fun, for Jimmy doesn't take himself too seriously yet takes his art very seriously. I know of no one who can equal his work ethic, his self-discipline, his command of his craft and his sense of humour. In a business that has more than its share of 'bad guys', he is one of that exclusive coterie of 'good guys', respected and admired for his humanity as well as for his comedic and dramatic skills.

If you're an aspiring writer who has bought this book to learn about writing from a master, you've made a good investment. Read on and immerse yourself in the advice offered by a consummate professional. And then, apply the seat of your pants to the seat of the chair, stop dawdling and sharpening pencils and making just one more phone call and reading your mail. Start typing.

Tell your story. Develop your characters. Don't hit the reader over the head with the obvious. Use economy with enough flourishes to give your writing your special style. Write dialogue that is true to your characters. Write scenes that advance the story. Let your audience *see* what is startling, serious, threatening, funny, mysterious, without telling them what's there before their eyes. Don't waste time on extensive camera or cutting directions; the director isn't going to pay any attention to you anyhow. In short, stop talking about it. Just do it!

And remember that, although there's little chance you'll be another Jimmy Sangster, there is, after all, the possibility that lurking somewhere in your future is – what else? – a Bentley.

Ernest Frankel
Los Angeles
June 2003

Ernie Frankel is a novelist, television writer and producer. A member of the Writer's Guild and the Director's Guild, he has been active in politics and philanthropy, is an environmental activist and was in charge of Management Communications on NASA's Apollo project.

A graduate of the University of North Carolina, he enlisted in the United States Marine Corps as a private and served on active duty as a combat officer during World War II. He was recalled during the Korean War and served briefly in Vietnam. He was awarded the Legion of Merit and retired as a Colonel in the Marine Corps Reserve.

He has held many positions on projects for CBS, NBC, ABC, independent production companies and the major studios, serving as creator, writer, executive story consultant, supervising producer and executive producer in weekly series and movies for television. The author of two novels – Band of Brothers, *published by Macmillan, and* Tongue of Fire, *published by Dial Press – he has won the Sir Walter Award in Literature. His work is included in Van Wyck Mason's* Anthology of American War Literature. *He has recently completed a new novel.*

Fade In

Opening Sequence

I never read a book on how to write a screenplay. I just sat down and wrote a screenplay. To this day I haven't read a book on scriptwriting. I've read the anecdotal-type books like *Adventures in the Screen Trade* that William Goldman wrote, 'my life as a screenwriter', stuff like that. But an actual 'how to' book complete with graphs and diagrams? Forget it!

Not that I'm knocking these books. On the contrary. When my publishers first asked me to write this one, I immediately went along to the local bookshop to check out the possible competition. There are dozens of them, including even *An Idiot's Guide to Screenwriting*. I leafed through a couple of them and I have to say I was impressed. I am sure there are thousands of people out there who've read Christopher Keane and/or Syd Field, the gurus of screenwriting manuals, and, in doing so, gained a vast amount of knowledge on how to write a script.

But as far as I'm concerned, any knowledge I've gained on how to write a script was, needless to say, through writing scripts. I was quite surprised to see how many of the 'how to' authors hadn't actually written a script or, if they had, it hadn't seen the light of day. But then, I guess you don't necessarily need to go to China to write about the Great Wall.

All this raises the question, would I be a better writer if I *had* read some of the 'how to' books? We'll never know. Apart from the fact that I'm far too old a dog to learn new tricks, I don't think books like that existed in my early writing days.

This leads to the next question. Will *you* be a better screenwriter if you read *this* book? Is it going to tell you anything you don't already know? I really don't know the answer to that one either. What I *do* know is that, having read this book and followed some of the basic advice I've tried to get across, you'll stand a better chance of selling your baby inasmuch as all the technical i's will be dotted, all the t's crossed. It will be around the acceptable length and the layout will be the way the potential buyer likes it, which is a lot more important than some people think. The spelling is up to you.

But remember, you will have written a screenplay using the style and technique that I use. Maybe if you read one of the other books, it would be slightly different in layout, emphasis, presentation, whatever. Not, I hasten to say, better or worse, but different. I can only tell you what *I* know, what *I* like, what has been successful and satisfying for me over the years. And make no mistake, I have been very satisfied and, without wishing to blow my own trumpet too loudly, I've been successful too. Have a look at my credit list at the back of the book.

There will be movies there that you liked and movies you disliked, the same with TV shows and novels. Unfortunately there will be a lot of movies there which you didn't see because you were too young and they wouldn't let you into the theatre way back then. Or, even if you *had* been old enough, maybe they were movies that you just didn't want to see. If there are, and you now want to see them, go rent them on video or DVD. Most of them are available. And I'm not plugging them for my own financial benefit. I don't get a cent. But if you are inclined to check up on me, please don't contact the Writer's Guild of Great Britain. I have a copy of a letter the general secretary wrote to an American author, Mark Miller, who was trying to get in touch with me way back in 1989.

Dear Mr Miller,

Thank you for your letter of 18th September. Jimmy Sangster is deceased.

Not even a "sorry to inform you" or a "regret to have to tell you".

But no hard feelings! I'll be writing about both the WGGB and the WGA in America later in the book. They are organisations that will be of enormous use to you. In fact, as far as the WGA in America is concerned, you can't do without it even if you want to. The studios all have contracts with the WGA, and they don't buy scripts written by non-members or, if they do, the writer has to become a member right away. And why not? Pension plans, medical insurance, you name it, the WGA provide it.

An early section of this book consists of a screenplay I wrote a couple of years back which I called *Fifty Fifty*. I went the normal route, which you'll be reading about, writing it 'on spec' and, after various submissions, the property was optioned for a year. They didn't get it off the ground, so after a year all the rights reverted back to me. It was optioned again, different people this time but same result. Back to me. (I'll tell you all about options later, the pluses and the minuses.) It's a script that I like. A piece of work which I am not ashamed to attach my name to. (There *are* some of those, which I'll tell you about later.) So I'm printing it up front so you can start off by reading it and then I can refer back to it in later chapters: 'why I did this' or 'why I didn't do that.'

One last word. The business you are trying to break into is a very tricky one. There is a lot of competition. The Writer's Guild in Los Angeles receives more than 40,000 original pieces of material per year for registration, which means that literally hundreds of scripts are written every month. Just check with the Guild if you don't believe me. That's where a lot of writers send their work to register their copyright. And while we're on about it, I strongly advise you to do just that. You don't have to be a Guild member and you can do it over the internet. It costs a few dollars, but it's well worth it in today's climate.

In England, the copyright automatically exists from the moment it is written, so there is no need to register it here although it can be done. Contact The United Kingdom Copyright Bureau, 110 Trafalgar Road, Portslade, East Sussex, BN41 1GS, or on the web at www.copyrightbureau.co.uk. However, if you haven't registered the property in the US you can't take legal action against anyone who steals it. Sounds complicated? It isn't as long as you remember to send it to the WGA.

As if all this wasn't enough, the market for freelance, uncommissioned screenplays is very small indeed both here in the UK and also in the States. But there *is* a market out there and let's hope this book will go a little way towards helping you crack it.

So... start off by reading the first section, then dive into the script. Maybe, when you've graduated to being a big-time producer (stranger things have happened), you can make me an offer for the rights. As of now, they're still available. Then you can rewrite it (see later chapters about rewriting) and, who knows, maybe it will get made and I'll be sharing a screen credit with you.

Read and, hopefully enjoy, the rest of the book. Some of the material you will be aware of or you'd not be fancying your chances as a screenwriter in the first place. But I think you'll learn a couple of new things which might be of use. Something else you'll learn about is me, the various ups and downs, ins and outs of my career. It's difficult to write about what I did without bringing up a lot of how I did it. So please excuse the odd autobiographical diversion.

And thank you for buying the book in the first place.

One

You've got to start with a story

Many many years ago, before I'd sold a thing, I sent the first chapter of a novel I'd decided to write to a man I knew, John Paddy Carstairs. I was around 17 at the time. I'd met Paddy during the war (that's World War II), when I was working as a third assistant director on a documentary he was shooting for the Admiralty. He was a successful novelist, a screenwriter and a director, currently doing his time in the navy.

"Please read this," I said. "And tell me if I can ever become a writer."

"What do you want to write?" he wanted to know.

"Stories," I said, not very originally.

"Like novels, short stories, plays, movies...?"

I couldn't answer him. As far as I was concerned I just wanted to be a writer. Where the desire came from, I've no idea. Neither of my parents were writers and, apart from Paddy Carstairs, I'd never met a real, true, died-in-the-wool author in any shape or form. But that's what I wanted to be and I wanted Paddy to tell me I had a chance.

He didn't read the piece I gave him. I can't even remember what it was. Perhaps it was just as well. He might have said it was rubbish and there was no way I was going to make it as a writer. But what he did say, which I shall pass on to you, is this: the only way to become a writer is to write... and write... and write. He also said that, if I was successful, I should dedicate my first novel to him. Fifteen years later, I did just that.

So... first part of lesson one... the only way to become a writer is to write...write...write. And if it makes you feel any better, you can dedicate your first screenplay/TV show/novel to me. The second part of lesson one is to *want* to write. To want it to the exclusion of everything else. Because, make no mistake, writing is an all-consuming task. That doesn't mean you can't have a day job... please God you have. Either that or extremely indulgent parents.

I had the desire to write and also I had a day job, which was just as well, because I didn't become a full-time, money-earning writer for another 12 years. I was lucky in that my day job was in the movie business. I was a camera assistant at that time, later moving over to the production staff as third assistant director at the old Ealing Studios. Then I did my bit for King and Country, came back into the business and climbed up the ladder, eventually to production manager. I was reasonably successful in all these jobs and I guess I could have hung in there and made a fairly good career out of it. But I wanted to be a writer, goddam it. And eventually I made it. Fingers crossed, the same thing will happen to you.

First things first. It's important to set yourself a regular schedule for your writing, be it two hours a day or 22. And if after the first ten minutes you haven't come up with a word that you can put down, *don't* say let's forget it for today and switch off your computer or typewriter. Stay where you are. Scratch your head; pick your nose; whatever, but stay put. You'll be surprised how suddenly something opens up. Setting yourself a time schedule is better that saying "I'm going to do five pages a day, come what may." I mean, it's great to do five pages per day, you'll have a finished script in less that four weeks. But it's no good putting something down on paper just for the sake of fulfilling the schedule you've set yourself. Better to finish the day's work with one good page than five indifferent and/or unusable ones.

So, third part of lesson one, set yourself a schedule. If you've got a day job, something which, at the start of your writing career, is advisable, then take a couple of hours in the evening or set the alarm for a couple of hours earlier than you normally would in the morning. If you don't have a day job then plan on a nine-to-five or a ten-to-six, whatever suits. But get your writing time organised or you're just not going to make it as a screenwriter or, for that matter, a TV writer or novelist... Poetry, I don't know about.

The fourth part of lesson one isn't so easy to arrange. The first time I went to Los Angeles I was around 45. I'd been in the movie business for 25 years. More, if one counted the couple of years I did before I was called up for my national service. Like I said, assistant director, production manager and eventually, at around age 30, a full-time writer. Anyway, here I was, a newcomer to Tinseltown. I was invited to a party given by a friend of a friend. The host was a Hollywood screenwriter with a couple of credits. Our mutual friend introduced us.

"I hear you're a scriptwriter from England," said the guy who was throwing the party. "How many scripts have you written?"

"Around 22," I said.

He wagged his finger at me. They're inclined to do that in America when they want to make a point. "But how many got made?" he asked.

I didn't know what he was talking about. "Twenty-two," I said. "What's the point in writing a script if it's not made?"

Which goes to show I was an extremely lucky guy. Nowadays it's "How many scripts have you written?"

"Twenty-two."

"How many got made?"

"Are you crazy?"

Back then, I wasn't crazy, I was lucky. I was in the right place at the right time. And this is the fifth part of lesson one: try to be in the right place at the right time. This is something I can't teach you, nobody can. Like any number of scriptwriting savants, I can tell you how to put together a shootable script... at least what *I* think is a shootable script... but that'll be as far as it goes. The rest is up to you... and your agent, assuming you've got an agent... and the studios who won't even read a script unless it is submitted by an agent and not always then... and the money men... and who's making what kind of movie at that particular time... and can you get an actor/actress interested and/or a director. And maybe I should shut up about here before you regret buying this book and start looking for another career.

Because, make no mistake, this is an absolute bitch of a business. And, as far as I can make out, it is getting worse rather than better. You often hear that Hollywood is full of young hopefuls waiting to be discovered so they will become movie stars. They pump gas, they wait tables, they package groceries. But for every young actor hopeful, there's a young writer hopeful. Some have been or are going to film school, some are taking a chance, having read a couple of screenplays and come up with an "I can do that" attitude. This applies to the UK as well as the US. It's just that in the UK the market is a hell of a lot smaller than in the US, which makes it even more difficult.

But before you despair, remember what Irving Thalberg, one of Hollywood's great producers, said way back in the 1930s. Mr Thalberg stated that "Writers are the most important part of the making of a motion picture." He then went on to spoil it a little by saying "...and we must do everything in our power to prevent them from finding out." But more about that later.

One other story that may be of some passing interest, and is certainly worth bearing in mind when you're feeling particularly full of yourself, and that is the importance assigned to the screenwriter by Joe Public. I was living and working in LA one time when the Writer's Guild went on strike. Every morning I'd call the Guild and they would give me my assignment for the day, in other words, the studio I was going to picket.

I'd drop in at the nearest coffee shop to the studio where I'd invariably bump into fellow writers who'd drawn the same studio. We'd have some breakfast, bitch about how hard life had become and what shits the studios were being, then we'd drive to the studio we'd been assigned to, ask their permission to use their parking lot, park our Cadillacs or Mercedes, collect our UNFAIR TO WRITERS signs and plod up and down outside the main entrance for the next two or three hours.

Walking the beat outside Paramount Studios one morning, a truck pulls up and a young guy gets out with a delivery for the studio. Polite, obviously a union-inclined man, he asks if we mind him crossing our picket line. No problem. In he goes to make his delivery. Five minutes later he's out again. He watches us for a moment, pacing up and down with our WGA signs. Then he comes over to me.

"You guys are on strike. Right?"

"Right," says I.

"You're writers?"

I agree that we're writers.

"So what do you write?"

"Television stuff mostly. Shows like *Columbo, Ironside, Mission: Impossible*."

"So what are you striking for?"

"More money," says I.

Long pause. Finally: "You mean you get paid for doin' that shit?"

So, assuming you still want to be a writer, let's get down to the nitty gritty. You've got yourself a schedule, you've got your fingers crossed that you're going to be in the right place at the right time, all that remains is to write the bloody thing.

I might sound as if I'm stating the obvious and perhaps coming across as patronising, but, as the chapter heading points out, you've got to start with a story. Let me say it again... louder:

YOU'VE GOT TO START WITH A STORY.

Down the line somewhere you can bury your story under a whole pile of characterisations, plot twists, whatever. But up front, there has to be a straight-line story. It has to be a story that grabs you, the writer, because if it doesn't, you're not going to be able to tell it in a way that will grab others, and by 'others' I mean first the readers, then the developers and, finally, if you're extremely lucky, your audience who have paid hard-earned money to be entertained. And, make no mistake, that's what we are trying to do. We're not trying to educate or enlighten, we're trying to entertain.

The story doesn't have to be long or convoluted. A straightforward 'Boy meets girl ... Boy gets girl'. That's your story. Except it isn't. It's only two acts. You need three.

In my opinion, and in the opinion of most other screenwriters, play-wrights, even, to some extent, novelists, you *must* have three. So, your story becomes: Boy meets girl. Boy loses girl. Boy gets girl. To put it in its most simplistic way... Act One: set the scene by introducing your characters and their environment, and setting up the problem. Act Two is where everything goes wrong and Act Three is when everything rights itself and the problem is solved/sorted, whatever. Next time you go to the movies look out for the act breaks, usually 30/35 pages for Act One, 85/90 pages by the end of Act Two and 90 to around 120 for Act Three... It may vary a little, but not much.

Act One contains the grabber. Let me rephrase that. The first nine or ten pages of Act One contain the grabber. If it doesn't grab the reader, he's not going to bother with page 11. Introduce at least one of your main players, set the time and the place of the movie, set the mood and milieu and, whatever you do, come up with something that makes the reader desperate to read on.

Let's take as an example, an idea followed by a storyline and see how the three acts are formed. And, to make it easier (for me, that is) we'll use a story that I turned into a script myself. I won't use *Fifty Fifty* here for three reasons. One is because you haven't read it yet; two, because we'll be taking it apart in detail later in this book; and three, I think it's not a bad idea to use a very early script of mine, rather than something I wrote much later. My first, as a matter of fact. Bear in mind, what we are discussing here is an original idea as opposed to one based on existing material because, let's face it, at this stage there's nobody going to ask you to adapt somebody else's work.

First, the genesis of the project. I was unit production manager at a company called Hammer Films. The company had just made a movie based on a TV series by Nigel Kneale entitled *The Quatermass Experiment*. It had been a runaway success at the box-office, slightly surprising everyone. So the immediate reaction was let's make a *Quatermass 2*. For whatever reason, Nigel Kneale wasn't keen at the time, so the company started looking around for another subject in the same genre, namely sci-fi. The two guys who ran the company, Tony Hinds and Michael Carreras, were tossing ideas around in my office one morning when I came up with the suggestion that, instead of the 'monster from outer space', let's examine the possibility of 'the monster from inner space'. I figured, as production manager in charge of the budget, it would be cheaper to dig a hole than build a space ship.

"OK," said Tony. "Monster emerges from the bowels of the earth. What happens next?"

"Don't ask me," I said. "I'm not a writer. Unless, perhaps it…"

"Better if it…" said Tony.

"How about if… ?" said Michael.

In half an hour we had the bare bones of a story. All that was needed now was for somebody to write the screenplay. This being Hammer, nobody was prepared to invest any money at this stage so Tony suggested I have a go at it.

"I'm a production manager not a writer," I said.

"You're not doing anything else at the moment," said Tony. "Go write it. If we like it we'll pay you. If we don't, tough!"

I checked that I'd still be getting my production manager salary, borrowed a typewriter and started to write. What we called it upfront I can't even remember, but the eventual title of the movie was *X the Unknown*.

What I started with was the bare bones. The pitch, if you like. It's used these days by writers to sell their basic idea in the hope that somebody will be so intrigued that they'll put up some money to develop the project. An American I worked with much later told me that the pitch is as few words as possible… but enough to make everybody desperate to see the movie. For example, the pitch for *Jaws* could be "How about a really scary movie about a 25-foot killer white shark terrorising Martha's Vineyard during the summer school holidays?" Or, for *Some Like It Hot*, "How about a comedy where two musicians witness the St Valentine's Day Massacre and are forced to join an all-girl band to escape the mob?"

Later, when you've finished reading it, try coming up with a pitch for *Fifty Fifty*. Remember, keep it short and descriptive enough so everyone will want to see the movie…

Having done that, try reducing *your* storyline to a pitch and see what it sounds like. I was told that the pitch should be short enough to appear in *TV Guide* when the movie is screening on TV. Short, succinct and leaving the reader wanting more. Steven Spielberg was quoted as saying "If a person can tell me the idea in 25 words or less, it's going to make a pretty good movie." And he should know.

For *X the Unknown*, the pitch was simply "A monster from the earth's core creates havoc and mayhem when it bursts through the crust to the earth's surface." I admit, it doesn't sound like much these days, but back then it was enough to get the project going, which is the object of the exercise.

Next came the basic storyline and, hopefully, this is where the three acts start to take shape. In this case…

Act One: Strange goings-on in a disused gravel pit. Mysterious deaths, culminating in the monster, unseen and unidentifiable at this stage, breaking out and going on the rampage. We meet the main protagonists. The chief scientist who works in a nearby atomic power station and the army unit who clash with the monster on its first time out. At the same time, we plant the idea that maybe the monster is something to do with radioactivity and maybe it's searching for new sources of energy which can be found at the local atomic power station. How the hell are we going to deal with it?

Act Two: A couple of ideas fall flat as the threat grows, with the monster causing havoc every time it reappears above ground. Finally... our hero comes up with a do-or-die solution. Either it works or the whole world is doomed.

Act Three: the final destruction of the monster.

And that was basically it. Next came the treatment. More of which later. First I want to give you another example of the three-act structure, this time dealing with what, at first, seems like a far more complex plot line. I'm referring to the screenplay I wrote based on Bram Stoker's *Dracula*. This was also very early in my writing career. The third movie I wrote.

Although a great number of people have seen the *Dracula* movie, I doubt that many have read the novel. Published in 1897, it runs to around 500 pages and the story is told entirely through diary entries and letters to and from the various characters. In other words, a novel told in the first person by around six different people.

It opens with Jonathan Harker's journal, a day-by-day diary of what he is doing. He is, in fact, a lawyer, based in Exeter, but as the book opens he is on his way to Castle Dracula in Transylvania with legal papers that need to be discussed with the Count, who has just purchased a large house in London. En route he is warned by some local villagers to turn back. If he values his life, not to go to the castle. This gives the reader a sense of impending threat. He arrives. The Count is affable, a great host. All seems fine until Harker starts to notice some peculiarities. For example, there are no servants in the place; the Count never dines with his guest; he also has 'business' outside the castle every night; he never appears until the end of the day.

Things get worse and worse until, finally, Dracula departs the Castle bound for London, leaving Jonathan in the hands of three vampire women. Also in this act, we've learned a lot from Jonathan's diary entries about the people in his life back home, people who will be carrying the story forward in the subsequent acts. To smooth this transition, there's a brief exchange of letters between some of these characters as Harker's diary concludes.

So, what have we achieved in this act? We've introduced the main character of the piece, Count Dracula, and shown exactly who and what he is. And we've also introduced the other protagonists.

Act Two begins with the arrival of Dracula in England and the start of the mayhem he causes. The character of Van Helsing is introduced here, and the whole act is basically his investigation into what is taking place.

Act Three consists of the 'chase' sequence. Our heroes track down and eventually find Dracula, and destroy him.

And that's it. Acts One, Two and Three. But, as I said earlier, the book is a long one and the main problem up front was to simplify the storyline. Remember, I had to deliver the whole story in 90 minutes. (In fact, the final screen version ran only 82.) I did this by eliminating a lot of the subsidiary characters. Anybody who saw the movie will no doubt remember that I didn't bring the Count to England either. In this case it wasn't because it made the storyline more straightforward but because of budget restrictions placed on me by the production company. No way was Hammer Films going to go with a ship, at sea, at night, in a storm... forget it. Sure, have Dracula leave the country. He can cross a border between Transylvania and Ruritania by horse and carriage as long as it can all be shot at Bray Studios...

So what was basically an elaborate, convoluted book, narrated from at least six different viewpoints, became a straight-line story. For better or worse? I don't know. Many years later, Francis Coppola made his version of the book. He took over two hours to tell what was virtually the same story. I guess for devotees of the Bram Stoker novel, this version was far better value. As for me, I liked my version better. But then I would.

One last word about the first Dracula movie that I wrote... *Dracula* in England, *Horror of Dracula* in America. It was released in 1957 to an outcry of criticism.

"I came away revolted and outraged..."

"I can't remember being so revolted by a film..."

"I feel inclined to apologise to all decent Americans for sending them a work in such sickening bad taste..."

The film was released again in 1996 as part of a Hammer season at the Barbican Centre. Once again the critics reviewed it.

"Romantic cinema that transcends genre... unimpeachable and unsurpassed... a fine film."

I am bringing this up as an example of the changes of taste in the movie business. When I originally wrote *Dracula* and *The Curse of Frankenstein* they were classified as horror films. X certificate in UK cinemas, nobody under the age of 16 allowed in. Then came what I call the 'slasher' movies, more and more blood and guts. I'm not knocking them, I hasten to say. I don't particularly *enjoy* them, but most of them are well made and, to vast audiences of young people, entertaining. But what it has done is to force us to reclassify those early Gothic horrors that Hammer made. I now describe them as 'fairy stories' – "Once upon a time in an old castle on the top of a hill lived a wicked Baron..."

But going back to the importance of the three-act structure. As the late great Billy Wilder said, "If there's a problem with the third act, the real problem is in the first." He also said, which is worth bearing in mind too, that "The second act curtain starts the end of the movie."

So, having settled on your story, break it down into three acts. If the story is a good one, you'll find this isn't as difficult as it might at first sound. If it *does* prove difficult, there may be something basically wrong with the story. And breaking down into acts doesn't mean finishing Act One, fade out, start Act Two. The acts can drift into each other with a slight overlap between them. In other words, you can start Act Two a couple of pages before you end Act One. As I pointed out in the *Dracula* story, the end of Act One is interlaced with letters that introduce the characters who take over the story in Act Two.

Basically what I am trying to get across here is that by far the most important element of the script is its structure. We'll deal with the dialogue and the characters later. But if the structure isn't right, forget it and start again...

But having said all that at great length, there *are* people who no longer adhere to the three-act structure, who have gone beyond that. Woody Allen, for example. Check out a couple of his later movies, then watch *Annie Hall* again. But you're not Woody Allen. You may be his equal one day, but right now stick to the three-act structure.

So how come, you may ask, did someone like me manage to get the first movie I wrote into production? No previous experience as a writer, no instruction books or seminars. I think the main reason was that I knew the production side of the film business backwards. I'd been assistant director on more than 25 movies, production manager on half a dozen. I'd broken down, scheduled and budgeted the scripts. I'd even come up with suggestions for script alterations when, as a production manager, I thought something was going to be too expensive to shoot so maybe we could do it that way instead and save a few quid. Sometimes we could, sometimes we couldn't. But, the point is, I knew everything I needed to know about screenplays.

Also I was extremely lucky in the guys I was working for. Tony Hinds and Michael Carreras. Tony, who, as well as a producer, was a writer himself, said he liked to employ me as a writer because, apart from being a good friend, I always did what he told me to. Obviously he told me to do the right things.

One short anecdote about Hammer to finish up. After the huge success of the first Frankenstein movie that I wrote for them, Sir James Carreras, who owned the company, came up with a title: *The Revenge of Frankenstein*. He had an extremely talented artist design a blood-curdling poster, which he took to America where he announced it was going to be Hammer's next movie, starting shooting in ten weeks. Everybody wanted in on the act, which was the object of the exercise. If something is successful, let's make a sequel. Or, in the case of *Star Wars*, two sequels followed by three prequels. (Talk about milking a product.) Anyway, back to Frankenstein Two. The money appeared and Sir James returned to London and presented me with the poster. We start shooting in ten weeks, he told me, when can you deliver a script?

"But I killed Frankenstein off in the last picture," I reminded him.

"You're a writer. You'll think of something," he said.

And I guess that's what writers do.

So take an hour or so and read *Fifty Fifty*. It's not the greatest script in the world; if it had been, I'd have sold it. But it's enough for me to use as an example of plotting, which you've been reading about, and about character and dialogue, which you'll get to later.

Two

Fifty Fifty

FIFTY FIFTY

SCREENPLAY
by
Jimmy Sangster

FADE IN:

EXT. HOUSE - BEVERLY HILLS -- NIGHT

We are up one of the roads off Coldwater Canyon; the house is
a two floor, middle of the market property. A driveway with
room for around four cars and a two car garage connected to
the house. There are three cars parked out front right now and
the house is ablaze with light. We can just hear the sound of
raised voices coming from the house.

INT. HOUSE - NIGHT - ANGLE AT TOP OF STAIRS
Two people. LINDA and JEFF TYLER. Linda is an attractive, rangy
looking woman. A two year old face lift gives her a slight wind
tunnel look. She's also, in her time, had a tummy tuck, breast
implant and liposuction. She's around 40 but would never admit
to being more than 35 and then only under extreme pressure.
She can be sexy, provocative and charming but her natural
inclinations are predatory. She makes no move, takes no
decisions without first asking the question, "What's in it for
Linda?" She works, on and off, as a real estate salesperson.
She is bonded to a vicious little poodle named Booful.
Basically, she's a typical Beverly Hills princess.

Jeff is 45 years old. He runs a construction outfit. Mostly his
company does work for the Beverly Hills/Malibu set, doing add
ons, conversions, building guest houses, remodelling ...
whatever. He has reliable crews, so there is not often need for

him to visit the sites while work is in progress. His main task
is to search out and negotiate the next few jobs. The work his
people do is good and not overpriced, so word of mouth keeps him
pretty busy. He's bright, slightly neurotic and over imaginative.
He screws around and is inclined to drink too much.

Right now, the two of them are standing at the top of the
stairs having the grandaddy of all fights.

> LINDA
> How dare you come barging in like you own
> the place?

> JEFF
> I do own the place. Remember.

> LINDA
> Me too. Mr and Mrs husband and wife.

> JEFF
> That's a laugh, for openers.

> LINDA
> You weren't supposed to be here tonight.

> JEFF
> No shit.

> LINDA
> Santa Barbara. You told me you were going
> to sleep over in Santa Barbara.

> JEFF
> So I changed my mind.

> LINDA
> Little Miss big tits wasn't available
> tonight. Right?

> JEFF
> I don't know what the hell you're talking
> about.

> LINDA
> Ha!

Now, from upstairs, comes a guy, dragging on his jacket. His
name is MARVIN LEIDERMAN. About five years older than Jeff,
he's short, squat and aggressive. He makes to walk past the two
of them, but Jeff bars his way.

                    JEFF
          Bastard!

                    MARVIN
          You're supposed to be in San Diego.

                    JEFF
          I'm supposed to be in Santa Barbara, but
          I'm not there either.

                    MARVIN
          I suppose you're gonna make some big deal
          out of this.

                    JEFF
          Bet your ass.

And he hauls off and hits Marvin. The blow lands more by luck
than judgment, leaving Jeff nursing bruised knuckles and Marvin
with blood streaming from his nose.

                    JEFF
          Is that big enough for you?

                    MARVIN
          Shit! I think you broke my nose.

                    JEFF
          Gee! I'm real sorry! Let's just make sure...

Jeff goes to hit him again.. As he does so, Booful, Linda's
beribboned poodle, goes for him. He's so busy trying to fend
off the dog that Marvin is able to land one on him. It's not a
particularly accurate punch, but it catches Jeff off balance
and he hits the deck. Linda grabs Marvin's arm.

                    LINDA
          Better you get out of here. Call me later.

Reluctantly, Marvin starts off down the stairs mumbling dire
threats.

                    MARVIN
          Crazy asshole. Lucky I don't have you up
          for assault. Could be scarred for life...

                    LINDA
              (calling after him)
          Don't bleed on the carpet!

                              25

Jeff starts to climb to his feet as Booful continues to
gnaw away at his ankle. Now he kicks her clear across
the landing. Linda runs over and gathers the dog into her
arms.

                    LINDA
Poor baby. Izzooalrightthen.
   (to Jeff)
That's it. Out!

                    JEFF
This is my house, lady!

                    LINDA
Tell it to my lawyer.

                    JEFF
You don't have a lawyer.

                    LINDA
Sure I do. You just busted his nose.

                    JEFF
You were fucking your lawyer! I don't
believe it.

                    LINDA
He wasn't my lawyer until ten seconds ago.
But right now I can't think of anyone more
inclined to take you to the cleaners.

                    JEFF
It'll take a smarter son of a bitch than
him to get anything out of me.

                    LINDA
Dream on, asshole!

And turning, she heads for her bedroom, slamming the door
behind her.

EXT. TENNIS COURT -- DAY

A game of doubles tennis on the roof of one of the high rises
so we see Beverly Hills and/or Century City all around us. Jeff
is partnering a guy of similar age, name of MARTY. They're just
crossing over after game five.

                    JEFF
You're my lawyer, for Christ's sake.

>   MARTY
> In my office I'm your lawyer. Right now I'm
> your tennis partner.

>   JEFF
> Fifty per cent?

>   MARTY
> Right down the middle.

>   JEFF
> Middle of what?

>   MARTY
> Of everything. Past, present and, in the
> case of work already in progress, future.

>   JEFF
> That's crazy!

>   MARTY
> It's also the law. Now for Christ's sake,
> play some tennis. I've got fifty bucks
> riding on this game.

INT. CHANGING ROOM -- DAY

A little time later. Marty is just paying off his losses. Now
he joins Jeff.

>   MARTY
> You played like a spastic asshole today.
> Did you know that!

>   JEFF
> Why should it cost me?

>   MARTY
> It didn't. It cost me. Fifty bucks to a guy
> I beat on a regular basis. I've gotta tell
> you, I'm really pissed off.

>   JEFF
> I'm not talking about your crappy fifty.
> I'm talking about me and Linda. Shit! I
> caught her in bed ... my bed ... with some
> creep who lives up the hill from us ...
> her. Now I find out she's been banging him
> for the past six months. Every time I set
> foot outside the house.

> MARTY
> Come on! This is California man. Don't
> try telling me this is the first time
> you've heard of the community property
> law.

> JEFF
> I've heard about dying too ... but it's
> something that happens to other people.
> Something I don't intend to get involved
> with.

> MARTY
> Maybe you'd be better off. I've heard from
> her lawyer already. He's one tough son of a
> bitch.

> JEFF
> He's the guy she was in bed with. I slugged
> him.

> MARTY
> That could cost you another ten, fifteen
> grand.

Jeff shakes his head. He still can't quite comprehend it.

> JEFF
> Half?

> MARTY
> Around a million.

> JEFF
> You're crazy!

> MARTY
> Think about it. There's the house,
> furniture, the cars, your pension plans,
> your investments. They add up, buddy.

> JEFF
> You trying to tell me I'm a millionaire!

> MARTY
> You were a millionaire, before you started
> fucking around.

> JEFF
> She's the one who's fucking around.

                    MARTY
        She's the one who got caught fucking
        around. Maybe if she hadn't found out about
        you and what's her name ...

                    JEFF
        Wanda.

                    MARTY
        Montecito. Right?

                    JEFF
        That's Sandy. Wanda's Santa Barbara.
            (Pause.)
        But it's different for me.

                    MARTY
        Why's it different?

                    JEFF
        I'm a guy, for Christ's sake. Guys ... well
        ... it's OK for guys."

                    MARTY
        It's still gonna cost you half. She's a
        director of the corporation isn't she?

                    JEFF
        In name only.

                    MARTY
        Yeah! Well she gets half of that too.

                    JEFF
        Half of my business?

                    MARTY
        That's the law, old buddy.

Jeff thinks on this a moment.

                    JEFF
        She wants half the business, she'll get
        half the business.

He starts away.

                    MARTY
        We on for a game tomorrow morning?

>   JEFF
>   I'll be busy tomorrow morning.

EXT. HOUSE -- DAY

Early morning and Jeff is just supervising the last of some
very heavy equipment, bulldozers, forklifts etc, which are
being parked in the drive of the house. Bumper to bumper they
fill the whole space. Now the driver of the last bulldozer, a
longtime employee name of EDDY, gets down and comes over to
Jeff.

>   EDDY
>   That it?

>   JEFF
>   That's it, Eddy.

Eddy looks back at the drive, solid with heavy equipment.
Back to Jeff.

>   EDDY
>   You sure you know what you're doin' boss?
>   Me and the guys can shift 'em out in no
>   time flat. We're gonna need some of that
>   equipment later this week for the Malibu
>   job.

>   JEFF
>   Don't worry about it. You go on 'n get back
>   to work. I'll see you later.

Eddy looks at him a further beat.

>   EDDY
>   Yeah! Sure!

Then, with a shrug, he climbs into a minibus holding half a
dozen other guys and they pull away.

ANGLE ON BUS

As it goes down the hill and makes the first bend, we PICK UP
Linda in her designer jogging outfit as she returns from her
morning jog. Booful scampers alongside her. We HOLD ON Linda as
she turns into the last stretch before reaching the house.

NEW ANGLE

The first thing she sees is Jeff, leaning up against his car,

which is parked in the road opposite the driveway. It isn't
until she draws level with the drive that she sees the heavy
equipment. She stops, still slightly breathless from her run.
A moment, then she shakes her head.

                    LINDA
          Smart! Real smart! You gonna tell me or
          should I just try a guess?

                    JEFF
          It's your half ... some of it. The rest
          will be up later.

She looks from him, to the equipment, back to him. Then she
takes her mobile phone from the belt of her joggers and punches
in a number.

                    LINDA
             (into phone)
          Marvin - get your ass down here ... Now!
          Better bring the cops with you.

She kills the line. Looks at Jeff.

                    LINDA
          See you in jail, fuckface.

She starts to thread her way through the heavy equipment
towards her front door. We HOLD ON Jeff looking extremely
self-satisfied.

INT. BEVERLY HILLS POLICE STATION - DAY

Jeff is just signing for his stuff at the front desk, watched
by Marty. Now he pockets his stuff and joins Marty as they walk
towards the exit.

                    MARTY
          Corporate law ... that's what I'm into.
          Next time you get into trouble with the
          cops, call someone else ... OK?

                    JEFF
          You my friend or what?

                    MARTY
          When you're behaving like a reasonable
          human being ... I'm your friend. When
          you're acting like a schmuck, who needs it?

They go out through the main doors.

EXT. BEVERLY HILLS POLICE STATION -- DAY

Jeff and Marty, as they come out.

> JEFF
> We'll sue for wrongful arrest.

> MARTY
> What "wrongful arrest"? You slugged a cop.

> JEFF
> I slugged that creep who's fucking my wife.
> I just kinda pushed one of the cops who
> tried to stop me. Shit, I hardly touched
> him.

> MARTY
> Let's hope the judge agrees...
> (He glances at his watch.)
> You wanna bang a ball for an hour?

> JEFF
> No!, I want to get shit faced, fall over,
> legless drunk.

INT. BAR - NIGHT

It's a dark, serious drinking type bar. Jeff is just coming out
of the GENTS, and he looks like he's well on the way to
achieving his ambition... shitfaced, fallover, legless drunk.
He staggers back to his place at the bar, maneuvering himself
back onto his stool.

> JEFF
> You wanna know something, friend...

The BARTENDER looks like he couldn't care less. Shit, he's
heard it all before, twenty times over.

> BARTENDER
> You're getting a divorce...

> JEFF
> Hey ... how'd you know that? Does it
> show?

> BARTENDER
> You told me. Three times.

                    JEFF
          Is that right? You wanna know what I think?

                    BARTENDER
          Tell me.

                    JEFF
          Maybe we should have had kids. We talked
          about it before we got married. But we
          decided ... no crumb snatchers. Babies...
          who needs 'em?

He empties his glass.

                    JEFF
          Maybe ... shit, who knows! If things had
          worked out different we mighta had a whole
          houseful of the little bastards by now.

He takes a swallow from his empty glass.

                    JEFF
          Someone's been at my drink.

To the guy sitting next to him at the bar, call him STEVE.

                    JEFF
          You been at my drink?

                    STEVE
          Thanks friend! Jack Daniels straight up.
               (to the bartender)
          No ice. Got it! No ice.

                    JEFF
          Sounds good ...
               (to bartender)
          Me too. Jack Daniels up, no ice.

But the bartender's had enough.

                    BARTENDER
          That's it fellas ... out!

                    STEVE
          What out? Up, I said!

                    JEFF
          Me too.

                    BARTENDER
You've both had enough. You wanna go
quietly or you want me to call the cops?

                    JEFF
I already been in jail today. I'm on my
way...

                    BARTENDER
Gimme your car keys first.

                    JEFF
What?

                    STEVE
He wants your car keys.

                    JEFF
I heard what he wants.
    (to bartender)
What do you want?

                    BARTENDER
I want to keep my liquor licence. So gimme
your car keys.
    (to the Steve)
Yours too.

                    STEVE
Not mine, friend. I been here before.
    (to Jeff)
You been here before?

                    JEFF
I don' think so.

                    STEVE
I don' mean here here. I mean here in a
situ ... situ ... situation like this.

                    JEFF
Like what?

                    STEVE
Some bum takes your car keys. I been
here before. Three times ... no, I'm a liar
... four times. So I wanna do a little
light drinking I get me ... got me a
rental.

> JEFF
> Rental what?

> STEVE
> Rental auto.

> JEFF
> Still need keys.

INT. LIMO -- NIGHT

CLOSE on the face of a uniformed driver, GUS, looking into the back seat.

> GUS
> Where to, gentlemen?

ANGLE IN BACK

Jeff and the Steve.

> STEVE
> We're badly in need of a drink, Gus.

> GUS
> I dunno. You fellas ain't gonna be welcome most places I know.

> STEVE
> What about that place you took me couple weeks back...
> (nudges Jeff)
> ... get yourself laid at the same time.

> GUS
> Shit man! That's over the state line in Nevada. It's three, four hours drive at least.

> STEVE
> So who's in a hurry!

As he says it, he reaches between his legs and pulls a bottle of Jack Daniels from a paper bag on the floor. Holds it up in front of Jeff.

> STEVE
> You wanna bet ... keep us goin' 'til we get where we goin'!

35

                    JEFF
          Where we goin?

                    STEVE
          Friend ... we're goin' to heaven.

INT. SANDY DUNE -- NIGHT

This is a pretty lowlife joint just across the Nevada/Cal state
line. There are a few one arm bandits against the far wall, but
this is a brothel first and foremost so nobody comes here to
gamble. There is a bar area, with tables and booths. The place
holds a couple of dispirited customers and half a dozen rather
frazzled looking girls who are just sitting around. Jeff is
seated at a booth across from the bar. He is alone and there
are a couple of empty glasses on the table in front of him.
Now the waitress, PATSY, comes over. She is around twenty-nine,
pretty with a good figure, brassy hair and matching
personality. She's wearing a very short buckskin skirt,
Western shirt and a miniature stetson.

                    PATSY
          Y'all wanna fresh drink, honey?

                    JEFF
          Yeah! Same whatever.

                    PATSY
          How 'bout your friend?

                    JEFF
          What friend?

                    PATSY
          The guy you came in with.

                    JEFF
          I don' have no friends...
              (remembers)
          Yeah ... right ... he went off with some
          lady someplace ... I think.

                    PATSY
          I'll fetch your drink, honey.

She goes over to the bar to place her order with the bartender,
who we'll meet later, name of HARRY. We stay with Jeff as he
looks around him, bleary eyed. He is very drunk. Now, he starts
to try to pull off his wedding ring. He is still wrestling with
it when Patsy returns with his drink.

> PATSY
> Ain't nobody gonna give a goddam 'bout a
> wedding ring, honey. Most of our clientele
> are married or they wouldn't be here in the
> first place.

> JEFF
> I'm not married. Least, I'm married but I
> don't want to be. Can't stand the bitch.
> Hate her.

> PATSY
> Now don' y'all go talkin' like that.

She looks around then bends forward conspiratorially.

> PATSY
> Why don' you go over to that phone yonder
> 'n call your wife here 'n now. Tell her
> you love her. But don' tell anyone here I
> tol' you to do that 'cause it's bad for
> business 'n I could lose ma job, which,
> incidentally, is serving drinks, not pussy.

> JEFF
> You wanna know something? I wish the bitch
> was stone cold dead. If I was twice ... if
> I was two times the man I am ... was ...
> I'd do it myself...

> PATSY
> Do what?

> JEFF
> Under a car ... zap ... just like that. Set
> light to the house maybe. Drop a fucking
> rock on her head ... and her dog too,
> vicious fucking animal. Get 'em both with
> the same car... rock...

> PATSY
> C'mon! You don't want to go talkin' like
> that.

> JEFF
> Why not! It's true.
>   (downs his drink)
> 'n you can pour me another drink.

                    PATSY
        You sure, honey? Seems to me you got
        yourself quite a skinful already.

                    JEFF
        One thing they can say about Jeff ... Jeff
        ... Tyler ... that's me ... Jeff Tyler. One
        thing they can say about Jeff Tyler is...

He stops, having forgotten what it is.

                    JEFF
        How about that fresh drink?

Patsy gives up on him.

                    PATSY
        Suit yourself.

She heads for the bar.

ANGLE AT BAR

Harry, the bartender, is busy polishing glasses.

                    PATSY
        Same again.

Harry pours a straight Jack Daniels. He's a large, good looking
guy around thirty five. He's amiable, ambitious, but not too
bright. Him and Patsy have a vague on/off situation going on
between them.

                    HARRY
        He's really trying one on.

                    PATSY
        You know what he just told me?

                    HARRY
        He's crazy 'bout your tits.

                    PATSY
        No ... honestly ... poor guy wishes his
        wife was dead.

                    HARRY
        Yeah, well most of 'em come in here say
        that ... so's they don' feel so guilty
        'bout goin' with a hooker.

                    PATSY
          No. This guy's different. He really wants
          his wife dead.

Harry glances towards Jeff. Then, just as Patsy is going to
take the drink over, he stops her.

                    HARRY
          I'll do it. Hold the bar a couple of
          minutes.

He comes out from behind the bar, takes the drink and heads
over to Jeff's table. Harry in with Jeff's drink.

                    HARRY
          Hi, buddy!

                    JEFF
          Hi yourself ... tha' my drink?

                    HARRY
          Sure is. Mind if I sit a spell?

                    JEFF
          You can sit anything you like, friend.

Harry slides into the booth beside Jeff.

                    HARRY
          Y'all were talkin' to ma girl friend just
          now.

                    JEFF
          Just talking.

                    HARRY
          'n you said something 'bout you wishin'
          your wife was dead.

                    JEFF
          Yep! And you wanna know why?

                    HARRY
          Why?

                    JEFF
          Why what?

                    HARRY
          Why you want your wife dead.

                 JEFF
Right. Yeah. OK ... alive, it's gonna cost
me around a million dollars to get rid of
her ... you hear that friend ... a million
dollars ... shit, I didn't even know I had
money like that.

Harry looks around him. Leans forward.

                 HARRY
I'll do it for fifty grand.

                 JEFF
Right on! Do what?

                 HARRY
Take your wife out.

                 JEFF
You wanna take my wife out, be my guest.

                 HARRY
Deal?

                 JEFF
Deal...

He starts to his feet. Can't quite make it.

                 JEFF
You wanna give me a hand 'n point me to the
bathroom?

                 HARRY
Sure I'll give you a hand.

He starts to lead Jeff towards the gents when a very fat guy
overdressed in Western gear moves across. His name is MAC and
he owns the joint.

                 MAC
Toss him out Harry.

                 HARRY
He's alright boss, he just wants to take a
leak.

                 JEFF
Hi there pardner!

> MAC
> Out! 'Fore he throws up all over the
> carpet.

> HARRY
> What d'you want me to do with him?

> MAC
> I don' give a flyin' fuck. Just get him
> outa here.

> JEFF
> And a Merry Christmas to you too.

And so saying, he slips out of Harry's hold and folds up
quietly on the floor.

INT. TRAILER - DAY

We open CLOSE on Jeff. We don't see where he is, just that he's
horizontal and asleep.

> PATSY
> (voice over)
> Hey! Wake up!

Nothing from Jeff. Now Patsy leans forward into frame and. jabs
at him with her finger.

> PATSY
> Y'all hear me. Wake up!

Jeff's eyes open. Close again quickly. Then open once more.

ANGLE - WIDER

We see the place where he's been sleeping. It's a very messy
trailer. Stuff is everywhere. Whoever lives here is a real
slob. Jeff is stretched out on a bed with a rug thrown over
him. He's still dressed as he was yesterday and he looks
terrible. Patsy, on the other hand, is wearing jeans and a
shirt and very little makeup. She looks five years younger and
a lot prettier this way. Now. as Jeff closes his eyes once
more, she jabs him again.

> PATSY
> Y'hear me. Wake up!

> JEFF
> No.

                    PATSY
          Come on, you gotta.

                    JEFF
          I don't gotta do nothing. I'll talk to you
          later.
               (peers at her)
          Whoever you are ...
               (becomes aware of surroundings)
          Wherever I am...
               (sits up, wincing)
          Where am I? Who the hell are you? Jesus
          Christ my head hurts.

                    PATSY
          You wanna look out of this here window.

                    JEFF
          No.

                    PATSY
          Just look out of the window, mister.

Jeff does as he's told.

EXT. TRAILER PARK -- DAY

Their POV through window. It's a pretty grubby trailer park.

                    PATSY
               (voice over)
          See the green trailer...

INT. TRAILER -- DAY

Jeff and Patsy

                    JEFF
          I see it!

                    PATSY
          It's mine. Just as soon as y'all get
          yourself together ... you come on over
          there. We gotta talk.

                    JEFF
          About what? And who are you and where am I?
               (starts to remember)
          You're the cocktail waitress from last
          night. It was last night wasn't it? And I'm

someplace in Nevada. Right?

> PATSY
> We'll talk about it over coffee. Now get
> moving.

And turning she heads for the door. She turns back just before
she goes out.

> PATSY
> 'n try to clean yourself some. You stink.

And she's gone.

INT. PATSY'S TRAILER -- DAY

Open on Patsy pouring coffee and carrying it over to Jeff, who
is sitting at the table his head in his hands.

> PATSY
> Here. Drink this!

We see her trailer is similar to the other, but clean and tidy.
Jeff just continues to sit there, not moving.

> PATSY
> Drink your coffee. You'll feel better.

> JEFF
> It's too hot.

> PATSY
> You ain't even tried it.

Jeff takes a sip.

> JEFF
> It's too hot.

> PATSY
> So we talk anyway.

She sits opposite him.

> PATSY
> OK. What do you remember from last night?

> JEFF
> (suspicious)
> What did I do?

                    PATSY
        You got drunk for openers ... but that
        don't matter. It's what you did after Harry
        brought you home.

                    JEFF
        Who's Harry?

                    PATSY
        Ma boyfriend ... kind of. That was his
        trailer you woke up in.

Horror begins to dawn.

                    JEFF
        I didn't ... I mean ... me and
        whatsisname...

                    PATSY
        Harry.

                    JEFF
        We didn't ... did we?

                    PATSY
        Did you what?
            (guesses)
        Shit, man. No. Not with Harry anyway. He's
        straighter than a pool cue. Leastways,
        where sex is concerned. No. You made a deal
        with him.

                    JEFF
        Deal for what?

                    PATSY
        Man, you're somethin' else. You made a deal
        with Harry to take out your wife.

                    JEFF
        That's right. I remember now. He wanted to
        take out my wife. That's what he said. I
        think.

                    PATSY
        I must say, you're mighty calm about it.

                    JEFF
        No big deal. Anyone can take out my wife.
        And I mean anyone.

Patsy looks at him a long moment.

>   PATSY
>   Jesus! I don't mean take her out... like
>   ... take her out on a date. I mean take her
>   out ... like dead.

She grabs up a sheet of paper and shows it to Jeff.

>   PATSY
>   That's your signature at the bottom there.

Jeff looks at the paper bleary eyed.

>   JEFF
>   Could be.

>   PATSY
>   Could be, my ass. Read what it says.

>   JEFF
>   (reading)
>   I, Jeff Tyler, promise to pay the bearer
>   the sum of fifty thousand dollars soon as
>   my wife Linda Tyler is dead.

He looks at it a long moment. Then he reads it again.

>   JEFF
>   (reading)
>   I, Jeff Tyler, promise to pay the bearer
>   the sum of fifty thousand dollars soon as
>   my wife Linda Tyler is dead.

A long pause. Now he looks up at Patsy.

>   JEFF
>   Holy shit!

>   PATSY
>   That's a contract 'tween you and Harry.
>   He's very meticulous is Harry. He made you
>   a copy.

>   JEFF
>   You're putting me on ... aren't you?

>   PATSY
>   I wish I was.

Another pause.

>   JEFF
>   Holy shit!

Then he thinks about it for a moment.

>   JEFF
>   Harry. The bartender. Right?

Patsy nods.

>   JEFF
>   He seemed like a nice enough guy. I mean,
>   shit, he's not going to go around killing
>   people.

>   PATSY
>   Let me tell you about Harry. Harry's got
>   ambition. He's tried plenty jobs up to now.
>   Bartendin's just one of them. He's been a
>   swimmin' teacher. He's done gas pumpin'. He
>   tried training as a dealer in Vegas, but he
>   ain't too hot with numbers. He's waited on
>   tables, tried his hand as a cook, worked as
>   a carpenter, gardener ... you name it ...
>   Then a couple months back he saw this
>   movie. Goodfellas or Godfellas or
>   Godfathers or somethin' ... anyway, that's
>   when he decided he wanted to join the
>   mafia.

>   JEFF
>   Far as I remember, he doesn't look Italian?

>   PATSY
>   That's 'cause he's Jewish. But that's no
>   matter. He wants to be a "made man", which
>   far as I can figure means he has to knock
>   off a couple of people ... not for any
>   personal reasons you understand ... like
>   for money. A contract. And that's what he's
>   got with you. A contract. He'll kill your
>   wife, you'll pay him 'n he'll join the
>   mafia.

Jeff looks at her a long moment.

>   JEFF
>   You're putting me on.

                    PATSY
        I only wish.

                    JEFF
        That's the dumbest thing I ever heard.
        Please Mr Corleone sir, I'd like to join
        the mafia. You wanna let me have an
        application form, and here's my CV. See,
        I knocked off this guy's wife. Come on,
        lady!

Patsy moves over to her answer phone and hits a switch.

                    HARRY
                (voice over)
        I'm off to LA for a couple of days,
        Honeybun. Gonna do a little job on Jeff's
        old lady. Earn myself a reputation. Talk to
        Jeff if you wanna know the details, he'll
        explain it all and tell you where I'm at
        when he wakes up. He's passed out here in
        ma trailer. See y'all later.

The machine goes dead. Patsy turns to Jeff.

                    PATSY
        OK! Where's he at?

                    JEFF
        Jesus! I don't know.

                    PATSY
        You'd better start remembering, mister. In
        an hour or two he could be knocking on your
        wife's front door. Mornin' lady. Bang bang.
        You're dead. And please can I have ma money
        now Jeff old buddy.

                    JEFF
        I've gotta call Linda right away.

Patsy pretends to pick up the phone and dial a number.

                    PATSY
        Hi honey. This is your ever lovin' husband.
        Don' look now but I just hired me a hit man
        to blow you away. Y' all take care now!

                    JEFF
        So what do we do?

                    PATSY
        We get ourselves to LA fast and we find
        Harry before he does what he's gonna do.

EXT. FREEWAY -- DAY

A VW Beetle, Patsy's car, cruising down the freeway, Los
Angeles bound.

ANGLE IN CAR

Patsy driving. Jeff beside her.

                    PATSY
        You must remember something he told you,
        for Pete's sake.

                    JEFF
        Lady...

                    PATSY
        It's Patricia... you can call me Patsy.
        Everyone does.

                    JEFF
        I don't even remember being in his
        trailer.

                    PATSY
        He said you'd know where he's at.

                    JEFF
        I know what he said. I still don't know
        where he's at ... is.
            (pause)
        So how are we going to find him?

                    PATSY
        He's got a couple of friends in LA. I'll
        check with them. His brother lives there
        too ... someplace. But he don't get on too
        well with his brother.

                    JEFF
        We're going to have to split up. You go
        look for Harry ... I'll try to stop him
        getting to Linda.

                    PATSY
        How you gonna do that?

> JEFF
> Stand guard, I guess.

> PATSY
> From what you tell me she ain't gonna take
> too kindly to that.

> JEFF
> I'll just have to keep out of sight.

> PATSY
> Just keep an eye open for a beat up VW
> camper. That's what he's driving.

EXT. HOUSE - BEVERLY HILL -- DAY

Linda is just pulling into the driveway in her Mercedes
convertible. She parks and, getting out, she moves down to the
roadside to check the mailbox. As she takes out the mail, an
old VW camper, Harry at the wheel, pulls up close to her.

> HARRY
> Hey! Lady!

Linda turns to him.

> HARRY
> Where's Skyline Drive?

> LINDA
> Further up the hill, on the right.

She starts towards the house, checking her mail. Harry looks
after her for a long moment, before driving on up the hill.

EXT. MOTEL -- DAY

A small motel, someplace in the Valley. Maybe a dozen units.
Patsy is just coming from the office with a woman who has her
arm tucked in Patsy's. She's older than Patsy, a good looking
lady, slightly butch. They come over to Jeff who is waiting by
Patsy's car.

> PATSY
> This here is Marilyn. She's an old friend
> from way back. She owns the joint. This
> here is Jeff. We got two rooms.

She hands Jeff a key.

                    JEFF
          Yeah! Hi Marilyn.
               (to Patsy)
          You gonna take me to my car. I want to be
          at the house before it gets dark.

                    PATSY
          Sure!
               (to Marilyn)
          See you later.

                    MARILYN
          Come and have supper with me.

                    PATSY
          You got it!

Marilyn heads back towards the office. Patsy and Jeff towards
the VW.

                    JEFF
          Old friend?

                    PATSY
          Kind of. She was a hooker worked at the
          place I'm at. She got lucky and married one
          of her clients. Then she got even luckier
          when he up and died on her. Left her this
          place.

                    JEFF
          What did you tell her?

                    PATSY
          That you was my cousin from back East. I
          told her you weren't too bright.

                    JEFF
          Why did you say that?

                    PATSY
          Well... ?

She's looking at him. Finally he shrugs. They get into the car.

ANGLE IN CAR As they get in.

                    PATSY
          Soon as I drop you off, I'll start making
          the rounds.

                    JEFF
          It's going to be dark soon.

                    PATSY
          I'm not afraid of the dark. You gotta phone
          in your car?

                    JEFF
          Hasn't everbody?

She flashes him a look. Meanwhile she's started the car and it
pulls away.

                    PATSY
          Write down the number. I'll call you if I
          come up with anything.

Jeff scribbles a number on a scrap of paper in the glove
compartmnent.

                    JEFF
          I'm hungry.

                    PATSY
          Tough!

                    JEFF
          C'mon. If I'm going to be mounting guard
          all night, I need something to eat.

Patsy stamps on the brakes suddenly. Jeff nearly goes through
the windshield. She turns to him.

                    PATSY
          Listen, buster. It's your wife he's
          being paid to knock off. He succeeds,
          you're an accessory. You do heavy time.
          Right?

                    JEFF
             (pause)
          Right.

                    PATSY
          So stop bitching ... OK?

                    JEFF
          OK.

She starts the car again.

                         JEFF
            But I'm still gonna get something to eat.

INT. MARTY'S OFFICE. NIGHT

Early evening, the city lights going on outside Marty's very
plush office. Marty is just getting ready to quit work. The
phone rings. He hits the answer button.

                         MARTY
            I'm gone.

                         VOICE
            Mr Tyler's calling.

                         MARTY
            Put him on. Jeff?

                         JEFF
               (voice over)
            Yeah. Hey listen...

                         MARTY
            No, you "hey listen" buddy. We had a tennis
            date this morning.

EXT.BEVERLY HILLS - ANGLE IN JEFF'S CAR

Jeff, driving, on the phone and trying to eat a sandwich at the
same time.

                         JEFF
            Fuck tennis. I'm...

                         MARTY
            I'll make believe I didn't hear that!

                         JEFF
            Listen. I'm in deep shit ... I think!

                         MARTY
            I don't think I heard that either.

                         JEFF
            I'm calling you as a friend OK? Not as my
            lawyer.

                         MARTY
            Really deep?

                    JEFF
The deepest.

                    MARTY
OK. Not over the phone.

                    JEFF
What?

                    MARTY
All the phone's are bugged nowdays. You got
anything important to tell me ... face to
face. OK?

                    JEFF
If you say so.

                    MARTY
How about 10.30am tomorrow? Court 2 ...
we're playing Jim Barney and some jerk down
from Seattle.

                    JEFF
I'm not into tennis right now, Marty.

                    MARTY
Sure you are. See you man!

Marty hangs up. We stay with Jeff in the car.

EXT. HOUSE -- NIGHT

Jeff drives past the house, makes a turn, reverses, then parks
so that he can just see the front of the house form where he's
sitting in the car. He gets out.

ANGLE STREET

Jeff walks up towards the house, keeping in the shadows.
Finally he stops, looking towards the house.

HIS POV

Everything looks OK. Lights burning upstairs and down.
After a long moment Jeff turns and heads back towards the car
and gets in.

We see him lock the door and stretch out in the front seat,
ready for his long night's vigil.

INT. CAR

CLOSE on Jeff, eyes closed. HOLD for a long moment, then the
SOUND of banging on the window. He opens his eyes.

HIS POV -- DAY

Linda, face close to the window, is banging on it. She is
dressed in her jogging gear and has Booful in her arms.

                    LINDA
          Open the goddam window

Jeff lowers the window, still not quite together.

                    LINDA
          OK. What's it all about?

Jeff glances at his watch.

                    JEFF
          Jesus. It's seven thirty.

                    LINDA
          So? What are you hanging around for?

                    JEFF
          I ... I came to pick up some stuff. I
          didn't want to wake you.

                    LINDA
          Bullshit.

                    JEFF
          Bullshit or not, that's it. Now you want to
          let me pick up some stuff or you gonna give
          me a hard time?

          LINDA: Bet your ass I'm gonna give you a
          hard time.

She stabs out a number on her phone. She looks at Jeff while
the number is ringing.

                    LINDA
          You look like shit.
             (into phone)
          Marvin. Fuckface wants to pick up some
          stuff from the house. Do I let him? Yeah.
          Yeah. OK ... talk to you later.

She breaks the connection. To Jeff....

>   LINDA
>   He says OK but just personal stuff and I've
>   got to keep my eye on you.

Jeff climbs out of the car. Immediately Booful starts to snarl.

>   JEFF
>   Don't worry, I won't take more than fifty
>   per cent.

He starts towards the house. Linda follows him.

INT. HOUSE -- DAY - JEFF'S CLOSET

Jeff is inside the closet throwing stuff into a carryall.
Linda is standing in the door, Booful still in her arms,
watching him.

>   LINDA
>   That's mine.

>   JEFF
>   What's yours?

>   LINDA
>   That shirt. You gave it to me. You said it
>   looked better on me than it did on you.

>   JEFF
>   That was a couple of years ago. Things were
>   different.

>   LINDA
>   They sure were.

A moment's silence, both with their own thoughts. Linda gets it
together first.

>   LINDA
>   You can have the shirt.

>   JEFF
>   You keep it.

Another moment.

>   LINDA
>   Whatever.

She turns and moves away from the door. Jeff looks after her a moment, then he puts the shirt back before continuing to pack his stuff.

EXT. HOUSE - DAY

Jeff comes out of the front door with his carryall. Linda has just been to collect the mail.

>   JEFF
>   I left you the shirt.

A moment's pause. Now Linda toughens up again.

>   LINDA
>   Just because I let you in this time, don't
>   get any ideas.

>   JEFF
>   Like... ?

>   LINDA
>   Like thinking you can walk in and out any
>   old time. I don't even want to see you
>   hanging around ... OK! I do and you're
>   gonna wind up in jail again.

>   JEFF
>   You wouldn't be so free with your threats
>   if you knew what's going on.

>   LINDA
>   (suspicious)
>   What's going on?

>   JEFF
>   (moment)
>   Forget it!

And he heads for his car. She watches after him a moment before turning and going into the house.

ANGLE AT CAR

Jeff throws his stuff in the front seat, gets in, starts the engine and drives off.

EXT. STREET IN B.H. -- DAY

Jeff, driving further up the hill from where the house is.

EXT. VACANT LOT -- DAY

Jeff's car makes a turn at the top of the hill and stops next
to a vacant lot. Jeff gets out and moves to the edge of the
vacant lot, where he can see down towards Linda's house.

EXT. HOUSE -- DAY

Jeff's POV, looking down towards Linda's house.

EXT. VACANT LOT -- DAY

Resume Jeff, watching. Suddenly he hears his mobile phone
ringing from the car. He hurries back, opens the door and gets
the phone.

> JEFF
> Hello. Yeah ... hi, Eddy! What's the
> problem?
>
> No ... I can't make it out to the job
> today.
>
> You're gonna have to take care of it
> yourself.
>
> So we lose the rest of the contract, I
> still can't get out there. I'll talk to you
> later. Bye.

He breaks the connection and walks back towards the edge of the
lot where he peers down once more. Reacts.

EXT. HOUSE -- DAY

Jeff's POV. We can just see Linda's car backing out of the
garage.

EXT. VACANT LOT -- DAY

Jeff runs for his car, jumps in, and he's off.

ANGLE IN CAR

Jeff, heading downhill to tail Linda. His phone rings. He
answers it.

> JEFF
> What ... oh, hi! Any luck yet?

(intercut with)

INT. MOTEL ROOM - DAY

Patsy on the phone.

                    PATSY
I've called a couple of his old buddies.
Nobody's even heard from him. What about
you? Everything OK?

                    JEFF
Right now I'm following her down the hill
to god knows where.

                    PATSY
Stay close. We don't know what kinda crazy
scheme Harry'll come up with.

                    JEFF
Where you going to look next?

                    PATSY
I'm goin' round to his brother's place. I
spoke to Ron, that's his brother, 'n he
said he ain't seen hide nor hair of Harry
nor did he want to ... but I dunno ... he
may have been lying. I wanna take a look
for myself.

                    JEFF
Keep in touch!

                    PATSY
Sure will!

She hangs up. As she does so, there is a tap on the door and
Marilyn sticks her head in.

                    MARILYN
Fancy some breakfast, honey?

                    PATSY
I surely do.

She starts out.

EXT. SUPERMARKET PARKING LOT -- DAY

As Jeff drives in, Linda, who has already parked, is heading

into the market. Jeff finds a slot a couple of rows away and
parks where he can see the store entrance and Linda's car.
As he switches off the engine, his phone rings.

> JEFF
Hello! Oh, hi Marty.

(intercut with)

EXT. TENNIS CLUB -- DAY

An irate Marty in his tennis gear, on the phone.

> MARTY
Don't you hi Marty me ... in fact don't you
ever call me again ... OK ... never!

> JEFF
You called me.

> MARTY
A date we had! Ten thirty on court. Jim
Barney and his friend from Seattle.
Remember?

> JEFF
Sorry. I forgot. I've got some pretty heavy
stuff going down right now, Marty.

> MARTY
You told me. Deep shit, you said! You
wanted my advice as a friend and a lawyer.
OK ... here it is ... go buy yourself a
shovel.

He hangs up. We stay with Jeff...

EXT. SUPERMARKET PARKING LOT -- DAY

Jeff switches off the phone. As he does so he catches sight of
something.

HIS POV

A beat up VW camper has pulled in close to Linda's car. Now the
door opens on the far side, we see trainer clad feet hit the
deck and start towards the supermarket. We can only see the
lower part of the driver's body, jean clad legs. We
probably know it's not Harry because we've seen his camper
already and this ain't it, but Jeff doesn't.

CHANGE ANGLE

Jeff gets out of the car, runs round somebody who is just
trying to park, barely misses another car that is pulling out
and heads for the store into which the VW driver has already
disappeared.

INT. SUPERMARKET -- DAY

This is a big one; and it's busy. As Jeff comes in he starts
to look frantically for Linda and/or Harry. Up and down the
aisles; no luck. Finally he spots Linda with her trolley. He
looks round once more just to see if he can spot Harry and when
he can't he has no alternative but to approach Linda.

                         JEFF
               Hi! Small world.

She looks at him, a little difficulty in believing her eyes.

                         LINDA
               This had better be very, very good.

                         JEFF
               Yeah. Right.

He looks again up and down, almost as if he expects Harry to
suddenly spring out and murder Linda here and now.

                         LINDA
               So?

                         JEFF
               Yeah!
                  (idea)
               I changed my mind.

                         LINDA
               About what?

                         JEFF
               The shirt. I decided I want it.

She looks at him a long moment. Shakes her head.

                         LINDA
               You're sick!

                         JEFF
               It's my shirt.

                                LINDA
                I'll mail it to you.

And she moves away. Now Jeff has to keep watching her,
hopefully without her spotting him. He watches her as far as
the checkout then he ducks out another checkout point and out
of the store.

EXT. PARKING LOT -- DAY

Jeff comes out to where he can watch the front of the store,
which happens to be quite close to where the VW camper is
parked. He is so busy watching the store that he doesn't see
the camper driver approach from the other side and throw his
bag of groceries into his vehicle and climb in. At that moment
Linda comes out of the market with her trolley. As she does so,
the VW camper starts up. As far as Jeff is concerned, that's
it. The camper's going to run Linda down. He ducks out from
behind the car, runs to the driver's side of the camper as it
pulls out and drags the door open. We see the driver for the
first time, a big, mean looking guy.

                        GUY
                What the fuck...

                        JEFF
                It's cancelled. The contract's cancelled!

                        GUY
                You wanna leggo my door.

                        JEFF
                Listen. It's cancelled...
                    (twigs)
                Hey ! You're not Harry.

                        GUY
                No shit!

Now he hauls back and socks Jeff in the face. Jeff flies back
across the hood of another car. The guy slams the door and
drives off.

ANGLE JEFF

Flat across the hood, nose bleeding. Now, he struggles upright.
As he does so, Linda drives past in her car on her way out of
the lot. She doesn't see him. He is about to make for his own
car when the owner of the car he's been lying on arrives. He
looks at Jeff, then at the hood of his white Mercedes.

>   CAR OWNER
>   You've been bleeding on my car.

He looks around and spots a cop.

>   CAR OWNER
>   Hey! Officer. This jerk's bleeding over my
>   car.

The cop starts over.

>   JEFF
>   I'm sorry. OK ... ?

He starts for his car.

>   CAR OWNER
>   I just had her washed. Stop him, officer!

>   COP
>   You sir! Hold up there!

Jeff stops.

>   COP
>   You wanna show me some ID ... sir.

Jeff realises he's lost Linda. With a sigh he starts to dig in
his pocket.

EXT. HOUSE -- DAY

Linda drives up the street and turns into the drive.

CLOSE IN CAR

As she turns into the drive, she hits the garage door opener
clipped to her sun visor.

ANGLE IN DRIVE

The garage door starts to open. As it does so, we PAN off
shooting towards the road. We can just make out Harry's camper
parked a few yards down the street.

ANGLE IN CAMPER

Harry is busy videotaping Linda's arrival.

EXT. RON'S HOUSE -- DAY

Patsy's VW parked outside a small Valley house. In the driveway
there's a pick up with a sign on the panel BILLY'S POOL
SERVICE. Patsy has just rung the doorbell. The door is now
opened by a man in a T shirt and his undershorts. He's around
35, slightly overweight, with a wispy moustache and long, not
too clean hair. Not altogether a pretty sight. This is RON,
Harry's brother.

                    RON
          Yeah?

                    PATSY
          Ron?

                    RON
          Who wants to know?

                    PATSY
          I'm Patsy.

                    RON
          Oh yeah! You called 'bout Harry.

                    PATSY
          You mind if I come in a minute?

He looks at her a beat. Shrugs.

                    RON
          I still ain't seen him. But suit yourself.

He steps aside and she goes in.

INT. RON'S HOUSE -- DAY

Small, not too clean and not too tidy. A main room with kitchen
and doors leading, we assume, to a couple of bedrooms. As they
come in Ron heads straight for one of the bedrooms.

                    RON
          Sit yourself down iffen you've a mind to. I
          gotta get dressed for work.

He goes on into the bedroom, leaving the door open. Patsy calls
out to him.

                    PATSY
          You still got no idea where he might be at?

> RON
> (off)
> Like I told you on the phone. Me and my
> brother don't hit it off too good. Never
> did. Bastard was always beatin' up on me
> when we was kids.

> PATSY
> So you don't have an idea where he might
> stay if he came to LA?

> RON
> (off)
> Nope. What y'all want him for anyhow?

> PATSY
> He could be in a heap of trouble if I don't
> get to talk to him.

> RON
> (off)
> So what else is new!

Now he comes back into the room. He is dressed Western,
including the high heeled boots. He's just adjusting a stetson
on his head and walking bowlegged.

> RON
> How do I look?

> PATSY
> Just fine ... I guess.

> RON
> You was doin' a Western movie ... you cast
> me for a part?

> PATSY
> I sure would. I thought you were a pool man.

> RON
> Matter of fact ahm an actor. But parts are
> difficult to come by right now. A guy's
> gotta be on the ball. Today ahm doing this
> director's pool. Variety says he's castin'
> a new Western and I figure if he's at home
> and he looks out of his window while ahm
> there, ahm a dead cert to get a part. Might
> even get a speakin' part.

> PATSY
> Sounds like a good idea.

> RON
> Trouble, you said. Harry?

> PATSY
> Yeah.

> RON
> What kinda trouble?

> PATSY
> It's ... like it's personal.

He loooks at her speculatively for a moment.

> RON
> Stuck a bun in your oven, did he? Now
> claims he had a vastemectomy (sic) ten years
> back. Sounds like Harry. I'm right sorry ah
> cain't be of no help, little lady. Now if
> you'll pardon me, ah got me a coupla chores
> I gotta do before I go to work.

Patsy scribbles something down on a piece of paper.

> PATSY
> This here is my number in LA. You hear from
> Harry you tell him to call me.

> RON
> You got it.

He walks her to the door, showing her out.

> RON
> Y' all take care now.

He closes the door and immediately heads across to the second
bedroom door. En route he drops the piece of paper Patsy gave
him into a waste basket.

ANGLE IN BEDROOM

Ron comes in. This is the second bedroom and we can see by
some clothes strewn around that somebody is staying here.
Ron immediately starts searching. In 30 seconds flat he's come
up with a sheet of paper. It's the contract..

CLOSE

"I promise to pay the bearer the sum of fifty thousand dollars
soon as my wife Linda is dead."

                    RON
               (voice over)
          Holy shit!

ANGLE IN MAIN ROOM

Ron comes from the bedroom and over to his answer machine/fax.
There he copies the contract. Then, stuffing the copy into his
pocket, he takes the original back to the second bedroom.

EXT. RON'S HOUSE -- DAY

Harry's camper is just pulling in. Harry gets out and heads for
the house.

INT. HOUSE -- DAY

As Harry lets himself in with his own key, Ron is just coming
back out of the bedroom.

                    RON
          Hi!

                    HARRY
          Hi! Anything for me?

                    RON
          How could there. Ain't nobody knows you're
          here ... you tol' me.

                    HARRY
          Just askin'. Why you dressed like a farmer?

                    RON
          Ahm dressed like a cowboy ... and it ain't
          none of your business.

                    HARRY
          Suit yourself.

He heads into the bedroom. Ron follows him.

ANGLE IN BEDROOM

Ron comes in after Harry.

                    RON
          You wanna tell me why you're here?

                    HARRY
          I already did. I wanna change.

                    RON
          Job. Scenery. What?

                    HARRY
          Both. Maybe I'll try being a poolman.

                    RON
          A rich poolman.

Ron flashes the copy of the contract.

                    RON
          Fifty big ones.

                    HARRY
          Where you get that?

                    RON
          What do you care? I got it. Need any help?

                    HARRY
          No!

                    RON
          I'm gonna take half anyway ... so you might
          as well.

A moment, and Harry shrugs.

                    HARRY
          Suit yourself!

Ron's a bit surprised at not getting an argument.

                    RON
          You're up to somethin'.

                    HARRY
          The money ain't why I'm doin' it.

                    RON
          So why? What's this broad ...
             (looks at contract)
          ... Linda ... what's she to you?

>   HARRY
>   I don' even know her.

>   RON
>   So what for you're knockin' her off, if it
>   ain't for the money.

>   HARRY
>   Ain't none of your fuckin' business. Now
>   listen, I don't have time to hang around
>   talkin' all day. You want in for half,
>   you're in.

Ron can't believe it.

>   RON
>   Half! Like twenty five gees!

>   HARRY
>   Whatever. Now get off my back 'n go sweep
>   pools or whatever. I gotta go see a man.

He pushes Ron out of the room and slams the door.

EXT. MOTEL -- DAY

Jeff's car is parked alongside Patsy's.

INT. MOTEL ROOM -- DAY

Patsy is sitting on the bed watching Jeff, who is in the
bathroom checking himself in the mirror.

>   JEFF
>   I think he broke one of my teeth.

Now he comes out, a damp towel clutched to his swollen nose.

>   JEFF
>   He had a punch like a ton of bricks.

>   PATSY
>   Maybe so ... but right now, your wife has
>   got nobody standing guard.

>   JEFF
>   I've had it! You go watch her. Tell you
>   what, we'll take turns. But I can only work
>   nights. She spots me again and I'm the one
>   who's gonna be dead.

                    PATSY
          So if I'm watching your wife all day, who
          looks for Harry?

                    JEFF
          We'll rent a private eye.

                    PATSY
          Come on! Be serious.

                    JEFF
          I am being serious. We'll pay some private
          investigator to find him.

                    PATSY
          Do you know one?

                    JEFF
          Yellow pages.

                    PATSY
          I gotta better idea.

She goes to the phone and dials a number.

INT. SANDY DUNE -- DAY

Mac, the owner of the place, is behind the bar checking the
stock. He picks up the phone.

                    MAC
          Sandy Dune. Mac speaking.

             (intercut with Patsy)
                    PATSY
          Mac. It's Patsy.

                    MAC
          Hi darlin'! How much longer you gonna be on
          the trot? Ahm real short handed here.

                    PATSY
          Couple more days should do it. Listen, Mac,
          you know any private eyes in Los Angeles?

                    MAC
          What you up to now, girl?

                    PATSY
          Do you or don't you?

                        MAC
          Hang on.

He cups the phone and looks towards a group of his girls
who are sitting around one of the bar tables having same
food. They're not dressed for business yet so they look
pretty tatty.

                        MAC
          Any you ladies know of a private dick in LA
          who needs a job?

One of the girls, call her LOLA, answers him.

                        LOLA
          My uncle Barney. He's a private eye ...
          kinda.

                        MAC
          Is he any good?

                        LOLA
          What do you care?

                        MAC
          You're right! Talk to Patsy.

Lola comes over to take the phone.

INT. MOTEL ROOM -- DAY

Patsy on the phone, takes down name and number.

                        PATSY
          Yeah! I got it. Thanks Lola ... you're a
          honey.

She hangs up and tears the strip off the phone pad, holding it
out to Jeff. He takes it and reads the name.

                        JEFF
          Barney Godwin. Is he any good?

                        PATSY
          How good does he have to be? Ten more
          minutes and I'd probably found Harry myself.

                        JEFF
          I'll go see him. You get on up to Linda's.

                              70

They start for the door and out.

EXT. MOTEL -- DAY

Jeff and Patsy heading for their cars.

                    JEFF
          Take this in case you need to get in touch.

He hands her his phone.

                    PATSY
          What if you need it?

                    JEFF
          I've got another. Talk to you later.

                    PATSY
          Yeah! Right!

They get in their respective cars and drive off.

INT. ITALIAN RESTAURANT -- DAY

The owner, LUIGI, is setting up the tables in this small,
chianti bottle hung restaurant. Now he looks towards the door
as the light is blocked by somebody coming in. For a moment
the figure is in silhouette, wide shoulder padded suit and a
wide brimmed fedora. Then, as he moves into the light we see it
is Harry. Dark suit, shirt, tie, fedora. He looks like a
Sicilian pimp.

                    HARRY
          Signor Luigi... ?

                    LUIGI
          Yes.

                    HARRY
          Buon giorno.

                    LUIGI
          And to you, friend.

                    HARRY
          Parla inglese?

                    LUIGI
          What the fuck you think I'm doing! What do
          you want?

> HARRY
> You wanna tell me where I can get in touch
> with the local don?

> LUIGI
> Don? Don Johnson, Don Ameche, Don Juan? Don
> what?

> HARRY
> The don. The head guy. Like Don Corleone.
> Capiche?

> LUIGI
> What are you .... some kind of a nut?

> HARRY
> You don' wanna talk to me like that ... I'm
> gonna be a "made man".

> LUIGI
> A made man! What's that, for Christ's
> sake?

> HARRY
> You're Italian and you don't know what a
> made man is ...

He looks around to make sure the place is empty, then he
sidles up to Luigi and speaks very softly in his ear. A long
moment and Luigi backs off, looking at Harry like he was a
complete lunatic.

> HARRY
> So you wanna tell me where I can find the
> local godfather?

> LUIGI
> Sure I'll tell you. What's it worth?

> HARRY
> Soon as I get made .... five grand.

> LUIGI
> How do you get made?

> HARRY
> Once you done what you gotta ... there's a
> ceremony ... the godfather ... he swears
> you in ... somethin' like that.

                    LUIGI
          That's all he gotta do ... swear you in?

                    HARRY
          He's gotta slice his thumb at the same time
          I slice mine. We mix our blood.

                    LUIGI
          And when he's done that you pay me five
          grand.

                    HARRY
          That's what I said.

He starts to lead Harry towards the door.

                    LUIGI
          OK! You gotta go over into the Valley.
          Ventura Boulevard ... way out in
          Tarzana...

They get to the door and we don't hear the last few
instructions. Now Harry leaves and Luigi hurries back to the
bar where he picks up the phone and stabs out a number.

                    LUIGI
          Charlie ... you got any funerals on today?
          Yeah ... right now it's quiet in the
          restaurant business too. Listen ... reason
          I called ... you wanna make yourself a few
          bucks here's what you do. Get into your
          best workin' suit, borrow a hat ... 'n
          practice talkin' like Marlon Brando.
          Somehwere down the line you're gonna have
          to slice your thumb ... don't be such a big
          fuckin' baby ... it's only gotta be a
          little slice. So ... there's this guy on
          his way over to your place...

INT. VET'S RECEPTION -- DAY

Animal vet as opposed to military vet. The waiting area holds
two or three people with their pets in various stages of
distress. There is a reception desk and two or three doors and
a passage leading off. Now Jeff comes into the place. He looks
around and then checks the piece of paper he's carrying. He
must be in the wrong place. He's about to leave when the
RECEPTIONIST calls to him.

                     RECEPTIONIST
             Can I help you, sir?

Jeff walks over to her.

                     JEFF
             I think I'm in the wrong place. I'm looking
             for Barney Godwin.

                     RECEPTIONIST
             You're at the right place.

She hits a button on her intercom.

                     RECEPTIONIST
             Barney ... there's a guy to see you.

                     VOICE OVER
             I'm out!

                     RECEPTIONIST
             Too late. Don't worry. He's not a process
             server ... least, I don't think he is.

She looks up at Jeff enquiringly. He shakes his head.

                     RECEPTIONIST
             No he's not.

                     VOICE OVER
             OK! Send him in.

                     RECEPTIONIST
             Down the passage. End door on the right.

                     JEFF
             Thanks.

He moves off.

ANGLE IN PASSAGE

Jeff moves down the passage. Names on the doors. Doctor this
and Doctor that, Surgery, Pharmacy ... whatever. The last door
on the left has a sign: Mortuary. Jeff reaches it, realises
he's made a mistake, and starts back up the passage. As he
does so, the door opens and a guy sticks his head out. BARNEY
GODWIN.

                    BARNEY
      You wanna see me?

                    JEFF
        Mr Godwin?

                    BARNEY
        Come on in.

He goes back in and a moment later, Jeff follows him.

ANGLE IN MORTUARY

This is the mortuary for dead animals. On a table at back there
are three or four sealed bags, waiting for disposal. There's a
large ice box against one wall. As Jeff comes in, Barney is
just heading through a door at back. He follows him.

ANGLE IN BARNEY'S OFFICE

Very small. A table with a chair behind it, another in front
on which sits a very mournful looking basset hound. There is
a telephone and a small filing cabinet. The tiny window looks
out over a small bricked in yard where the vet keeps the
incinerator for disposing of their failures. Barney himself is
a large, untidy man around 50. His clothes don't fit any
better than the wig he wears. Why he wears it is a mystery.
Certainly not to fool anyone because he keeps taking it off to
scratch his head. Now, as Jeff comes in, he pushes the dog off
the chair.

                    BARNEY
        Fuck off.
            (to Jeff)
        You wanna sit down?

Jeff does so and the dog immediately clambers onto his lap,
slurping around the jowls onto Jeff's pants.

                    BARNEY
        Throw the bugger off if it bothers you.

                    JEFF
        I like dogs ... most of the time.

                    BARNEY
        Me. I can't stand them. What's your problem?

Jeff looks around the office quickly.

                              75

                    JEFF
        You are Barney Godwin, private investigator?

                    BARNEY
            That's me.

He drags a pad towards him.

                    BARNEY
            OK! What you want me to find?

                    JEFF
            His name's Harry...

                    BARNEY
            Dog? Cat? Goldfish? What?

                    JEFF
            A person ...
                (twigs)
            You're an animal detective. You look for
            lost pets.

                    BARNEY
            I'm good with people too. So tell me about
            Harry. Harry what... ?

                    JEFF
            I don't know if this...

                    BARNEY
            Listen. what's the difference .... some
            broad loses her fluffikins, she comes to
            me. Sometimes I find 'em, sometimes I
            don't. Take that creep you got there. Took
            me two weeks to find him. Custody battle
            ... fuck the kids, who gets the dog? Guy
            had hidden him to hell and gone. But I got
            there in the end. Problem is, now they
            decided they ain't gonna get a divorce
            after all and they don't want the dog back
            and I don't get paid.

                    JEFF
            So what happens to the dog?

Barney draws a finger across his throat.

                    BARNEY
            This afternoon.

Jeff looks down at the dog, who is looking up at him with an
expression of incredible sadness.

>   BARNEY
>   OK, where was we ... Harry what?

Jeff makes up his mind.

>   JEFF
>   Harry Bender. He lives in Nevada but right
>   now he's someplace in Los Angeles. I've got
>   an address here ... it's his brother's
>   place. We ... I ... couldn't get anything
>   out of the brother ... maybe you'll have
>   better luck.

>   BARNEY
>   What's he done ... this Harry Bender?

>   JEFF
>   Nothing, yet. That's why we need to find
>   him fast.

>   BARNEY
>   You gonna tell me why?

>   JEFF
>   No.

>   BARNEY
>   Like if I don't find him he's gonna commit
>   something pretty heavy.

>   JEFF
>   You could say that ... I guess. Here's the
>   address.

He hands Barney the slip of paper with Ron's address. Barney
looks at him a beat, shrugs.

>   BARNEY
>   Five hundred a day plus expenses ... take
>   it or leave it.

Jeff gets to his feet. The dog flops to the floor.

>   JEFF
>   (to dog)
>   Sorry.

77

              (to Barney)
          I'll leave it.

                  BARNEY
          OK. You twisted my arm ... four fifty.
          That's my last word.

                  JEFF
          Thanks for your time.

                  BARNEY
          Four... ?

                  JEFF
          Three.

                  BARNEY
          Deal. Where can I get in touch?

Jeff writes down two numbers.

                  JEFF
          That's my car. That's my mobile.

                  BARNEY
          Ain't you got a home?

                  JEFF
          Not right now.

                  BARNEY
          How about an office?

                  JEFF
          I'm not in the office much these last
          coupla days.

Barney looks at him long and hard.

                  BARNEY
          Maybe I shoulda stuck out for the five
          hundred. One more thing ... this Harry ...
          is he dangerous?

                  JEFF
          Not unless you happen to be my wife.

EXT. FUNERAL PARLOUR -- DAY

Harry, dressed as before, checks the address of the funeral
parlour, quick look up and down the street, then he goes in.

INT. FUNERAL PARLOUR -- DAY

Just inside the door, two guys in dark suits. Call them FRED
and BILL. Normally they're pall bearers. Right now they're
mafiosa. As Harry comes in they block his way.

>   FRED
>   Where ya goin'?

>   HARRY
>   I wanna talk with the godfather.

>   FRED
>   Maybe he don' wanna talk with you...

He nods towards Bill, who moves off through the coffins towards
a curtained area in the back. He disappears behind the curtains.

>   HARRY
>   Ain't you gonna frisk me... ?

>   FRED
>   Oh ... yeah ... sure... !

He pats Harry down.

>   HARRY
>   I'm clean.

>   FRED
>   Yeah.

At that moment Bill reappears from behind the curtains and nods
towards them. Fred gives Harry a little push.

>   FRED
>   OK.

Harry straightens his tie and walks towards the curtains.

ANGLE - ROOM

A few more coffins. One on a trestle. There's a chair on the
far side and in the chair sits a large man, wide brimmed hat,
face in shadow. When he speaks, surprise, surprise, he sounds
just like Don Corleone. Name of CHARLIE.

> CHARLIE
> What you want with me?

> HARRY
> I wanna be a made man.

> CHARLIE
> Issa gonna cost you plenty money.

> HARRY
> I'm getting the money ... pretty soon.

> CHARLIE
> I tells you what you do ... you getta the
> money 'n you come back here 'n I'll make
> you a made man, man.

> HARRY
> Don't you wanna know what ahm gonna do to
> get the money?

> CHARLIE
> You tell me later ... OK ... now I'm busy
> ... Ciao!

After a beat, Harry starts to back out. Stops halfway.

> HARRY
> I got a contract.

> CHARLIE
> Bene, bene!

> HARRY
> You wanna see it?

> CHARLIE
> Justa bringa me the money ... OK ... then I
> sign your contract.

> HARRY
> No ... the contract's mine ... capiche?

> CHARLIE
> Si ... si ... you go now. I see you when
> you got the money.

Harry looks at him a beat longer. Not quite what he was
expecting. But what the hell! Now he turns and starts out.

INT. RON'S HOUSE -- DAY

The doorbell is ringing. Nobody home. A long moment and then
the door opens and Barney Godwin comes in, sticking a bunch of
keys back in his pocket.

                    BARNEY
          Anybody home?

No reply. Barney comes all the way in, closes the door and
starts to look around. He peers into Ron's bedroom, then into
the one being used by Harry.

ANGLE IN HARRY'S ROOM

Barney wanders in. On the dresser are some video tapes. He
looks at them briefly, then he pulls open a drawer and looks
through that. Nothing of much interest. Now he takes one of the
tapes and heads back into the main room.

ANGLE IN LIVING ROOM

Barney goes over to the TV and video and loads one of the tapes.

CLOSE TV

A shot of Linda's house. Then a shot of Linda coming out and
collecting the mail. Later a shot of Linda outside a store in
Beverly Hills, then another of her at the house.

CLOSE - BARNEY

Watching the TV. Now he hits the pause button and moves closer
to the TV.

CLOSE TV

The street number of the house is clearly visible. Now the
picture advances slowly as Linda drives away, camera panning
with her. The picture is paused again as we are able to see the
street sign ... Belview Road.

CLOSE BARNEY

Not sure what to make of it. Now he ejects the tape and carries
it back to the bedroom.

ANGLE IN HARRY'S BEDROOM

Barney in. Replaces the tape. Looks around. Harry's jean jacket

is slung over the back of a chair. He goes through the pockets
and comes up with a sheet of paper which he unfolds.

CLOSE

The contract. "I promise to pay the bearer fifty thousand
dollars soon as my wife Linda is dead."

ANGLE BARNEY.

> BARNEY
> Wow! It's Christmas.

He heads for the main room once more.

ANGLE IN MAIN ROOM

Barney over to the fax machine where he faxes the
contract. While he's doing it, he picks up the phone and
punches out a number. He listens to it ring for a moment.
Finally...

> BARNEY
> Let me speak to Lola ... No, I'm not a
> punter, I'm her uncle.

INT. SANDY DUNE — DAY
Mac, at one of the tables, eating. On the phone. Now he cups it
and calls.

> MAC
> Lola ... phone!

ANOTHER ANGLE
Lola and one of the other girls are seated at a booth at back
playing Scrabble.

> LOLA
> I'm already booked up tonight.

> MAC
> He says he's your uncle.

> LOLA
> Now what?

She gets up and moves over to the bar where there is another
line. Picks up the phone and punches a button. As she starts to
talk, Mac hangs up his phone.

> LOLA
Barney ... how's with you?

>   (intercut with Barney)

BARNEY: Hi girl! What do you know about
Tyler?

> LOLA
Who's Tyler?

> BARNEY
The guy you told come see me.

> LOLA
I never told no guy ... oh yeah ... Patsy,
I told Patsy.

> BARNEY
Who's Patsy?

> LOLA
She works here. But she ain't here right
now, she's off in LA someplace.

> BARNEY
With Tyler. Right?

> LOLA
I told you. I don't know no Tyler. Less he
was the fella she took pity on the other
night ... bitchin' 'bout his wife ...
cussin' 'n swearin' 'n wishin' she was dead
'n all.

> BARNEY
That's him. Thanks girl. You have a nice
day now.

He hangs up. Looks at the contract again. Hums the first bar of
the song.

> BARNEY
We're in the money...

Now he takes the original back into Harry's room. A
moment later he comes out and heads for the front door and
out.

EXT. LINDA'S HOUSE -- NIGHT

A little way down the street is parked Patsy's car.

CLOSE PATSY

She's bored out of her twist, but she's doing her job
nevertheless, namely watching the house. So when Jeff comes
up behind the car and suddenly presses his face against the
driver's window, she nearly has a fit.

> PATSY
> You scared the bejesus outta me!

Jeff climbs in beside her. A moment later the basset hound from
Barney's scrambles in beside him.

> PATSY
> Jesus. What's that?

> JEFF
> They were gonna put him down. What else
> could I do?

> PATSY
> You put out a contract on your wife, but
> God forbid anybody kill a dog.

> JEFF
> It's different!

He tries to push the dog to the floor.

> JEFF
> Geroff!

> PATSY
> Where's your car?

> JEFF
> Back there round the corner. I brought you
> something to eat.

He hands her a wrapped sandwich. He's got one for himself too.
For a moment there is silence as the two of them unwrap their
sandwiches and start in. Occasionally he breaks off a piece and
gives it to the dog, who is sitting on the floor between his
legs dribbling on him.

                    JEFF
          Anything happening?

                    PATSY
             Nope.

Another silence.

                    PATSY
             Nice house.

                    JEFF
          I built it. That's what I do. I'm a
          builder.
                    PATSY
          I'm a singer.

                    JEFF
          Is that a fact?

                    PATSY
          Right now there isn't much work around so I
          sling cocktails to pay the rent.

                    JEFF
          What about you and Harry... ?

                    PATSY
          Me and Harry what?

                    JEFF
          Like together ... sweethearts ... whatever?

                    PATSY
          Come on! He's a nice guy, Harry. But let's
          face it, when you come down to basics, he's
          a coupla sandwiches short of a picnic.

                    JEFF
          I just figured, with you worried about him
          the way you are...

                    PATSY
          He'd like that. He truly would. I guess
          that's why I'm concerned 'bout him. Anybody
          feels about me the way he does ... then I
          just can't help feeling a mite responsible.

                    JEFF
          That's how I feel about this here.

                  (indicates dog)
           Soon as he saw me he knew he was onto a
           good thing.

                  PATSY
           Did you bring something to drink?

Jeff digs into the bag and comes up with a couple of cans of
beer. Hands one to Patsy.

                  JEFF
           So there's nobody in your life right now.

                  PATSY
           Nobody worth mentioning...

Takes a swig of the beer.

                  PATSY
           But don't go getting any ideas.

                  JEFF
           Me!

                  PATSY
           I can spot that look in a guy's eye from a
           mile off. I guess it comes from working in
           a whorehouse. Hey, we're getting some
           action.

Jeff looks out.

THEIR POV

Marvin's car is just pulling into the driveway. As it does so,
the hooter sounds. The car is still involved in turning around
when Linda comes out of the house.

CLOSE JEFF AND PATSY

                  PATSY
           That your wife?

                  JEFF
           Right. And that's the creep who's banging
           her.

                  PATSY
           Good looking lady.

                    JEFF
          Once upon a time.

He opens the car door.

                    JEFF
          I'll take it from here. You still got the
          phone?

She taps her purse.

                    JEFF
          I'll call you.

He gets out of the car and the dog starts to follow him.

                    JEFF
          You stay there.

                    PATSY
          Come on!

                    JEFF
          Stick him in my room at the motel. Give him
          some water and maybe stop on the way for a
          can of dog food. OK?

A moment. Then she shakes her head.

                    PATSY
          I guess.

He pushes the dog back into the car and closes the door. Now he
heads back towards where he's left his own car. Patsy looks
towards the house once more.

HER POV

Linda is just getting into Marvin's car. A moment later it
pulls away.

ANOTHER ANGLE

As Marvin's car heads down the hill, Jeff's car pulls out from
behind Patsy's and takes off after it. As soon as they have
gone, Patsy starts up and drives off, heading home.

ANGLE ROAD JUNCTION

Marvin's car pulls into Coldwater heading towards Beverly Hills flats. A couple of seconds later Jeff's car makes the same turn.

EXT. LINDA'S HOUSE -- NIGHT

We see Harry approaching on foot. He is carrying a small carryall bag and a roll of hosepipe. He looks off down the hill after the departing cars, then he heads into the driveway.

EXT. RESTAURANT - BEVERLY HILLS -- NIGHT

Marvin is just handing over his car to the parking attendant outside the restaurant. He and Linda go in.

ANOTHER ANGLE

Across the street Jeff's car pulls up.

CLOSE IN JEFF'S CAR

Jeff settles back, prepared to wait.

EXT. LINDA'S HOUSE -- NIGHT

The place seems quiet and empty. Then we hear a crash of sound and Harry's voice.

                    HARRY
              (voice over)
          Goddam sonofabitch!

ANGLE AT BACK OF HOUSE

Harry has just bashed his hand on the window frame he was trying to force open. He's nursing his bruised knuckles. Now, he picks up the steel jemmy he's been using and gets to it again. This time the window cracks open after a few seconds. Harry gathers up his roll of hosepipe and starts in.

INT. LINDA'S HOUSE -- NIGHT

Harry comes through the window into the dining room. He takes out a flashlight. It doesn't work. He whacks it on the dining room table and gets a light. Now he crosses into the hall, and starts up the stairs.

ANGLE - TOP LANDING

Harry comes up the stairs. He looks into one of the rooms leading off. Wrong. Looks into another and goes in.

INT. MASTER BEDROOM -- NIGHT

Obviously the master bedroom. King bed, lots of drapes, a small
desk to one side, a chaise longue, bathroom and dressing room
leading off. Harry looks around, shakes his head.

                    HARRY
          Some pad!

But now he gets down to work. First he heads across to the
window at the rear. He opens it, secures one end of the
hosepipe to the edge of the window frame and throws the
rest out.

EXT. RESTAURANT - BEVERLY HILLS

CLOSE on Jeff in his car, bored out of his twist, only just
managing to stay awake. Now he pulls himself together, looking
out.

HIS POV

Marvin and Linda, waiting for Marvin's car to be fetched.
Marvin looks a shade unsteady on his feet.

ANGLE JEFF

He sinks lower in his seat. God forbid Linda should spot him.

ANGLE FRONT OF RESTAURANT

Marvin's car arrives. Marvin is about to get in the driver's
side when Linda stops him.

                    LINDA
          I'll drive.

                    MARVIN
          Why?

                    LINDA
          Because you're drunk is why.

They get in and a moment later the car pulls away. Jeff follows
a little way behind.

EXT. HOUSE -- NIGHT

There is no sign of Harry. Everything seems quiet. Now Marvin's
car pulls into the drive. He and Linda get out and head for the

front door. A moment, and they're inside. PAN OFF as Jeff's car
cruises quietly by. It disappears down the street. A long
moment, then it reappears, having turned round. Now it stops a
few yards away where Jeff intends to spend the night keeping
watch.

ANGLE IN CAR

Jeff punches out a number on his car phone.

INT. MOTEL ROOM -- NIGHT

Close on Jeff's mobile phone as it rings. A moment and a hand
comes in and picks it up. WIDEN ANGLE to show Patsy, in bed
with Marilyn, who's sitting up, glasses on, reading. Also on
the bed is the dog, snoring gently.

                    PATSY
          Hello - oh, hi! What's happening?

               (intercut with Jeff in car)

                    JEFF
          Nothing. What are you doing?

                    PATSY
          I'm in bed already.

                    JEFF
          Any message from Barney Godwin?

Patsy looks towards Marilyn.

                    PATSY
          Were there any messages for Jeff?

Marilyn shakes her head.

                    PATSY
          No.

                    JEFF
          Who are you talking to?

                    PATSY
          Marilyn.

                    JEFF
          I thought you said you were in bed already.

                              PATSY
                    We are!

                              JEFF
                         (a moment)
                    Ah!

                              PATSY
                    I fed the dog.

                              JEFF
                    Good.

                              PATSY
                    Anything else?

                              JEFF
                    I guess not.

                              PATSY
                    Good night then.

And she hangs up. Jeff looks at the phone for a beat before
doing likewise. Now he looks towards the house once more.

HIS POV - THE HOUSE

Lights on upstairs. The rest in darkness.

INT. BACK GARDEN -- NIGHT

Harry now comes into the garage through the rear service door.
He goes to Linda's car and, hotwiring, he starts the engine.
Then he moves round to the rear of the car and looks down.

HIS POV

One end of the hose he'd been carrying is taped to the car
exhaust pipe. Now we PAN along the hose to where it goes out of
a window at the back of the garage.

EXT. BACK GARDEN -- NIGHT

We follow the hose across to the rear of the house and then up
towards the upper floor window where the light is on.

INT. MASTER BEDROOM -- NIGHT

The window that Harry had started work on. The end of the hose
is taped to the edge of a break in the window frame. The carbon

monoxide is pumping straight into the bedroom. Over, we can hear loud snoring.

WIDER ANGLE

Now Linda comes from the dressing room/bathroom area wearing a nightdress. She crosses to the bed and looks down at Marvin. He is still dressed except for his jacket, flat on his back, sound asleep and snoring loudly.

                    LINDA
          The last of the red hot lovers!

She grabs her pillow from the other side of the bed and goes out of the room, switching off the light as she does so.

EXT. BACK GARDEN -- NIGHT

Harry is standing in the shelter of some bushes. He sees the light go out, checks his watch, then heads back towards the garage.

INT. SPARE BEDROOM -- NIGHT

Linda comes in and starts to turn down one of the twin beds.

INT. MASTER BEDROOM -- NIGHT

Marvin, still snoring loudly. PAN OFF towards the window where the hose is attached.

EXT. BACK GARDEN

We follow the hose back towards the garage.

INT. GARAGE -- NIGHT

Harry is sitting in the front of Linda's car, the doors open, reading TRUE CRIME or some such magazine. Now he glances at his watch again.

EXT. HOUSE - NIGHT

Close on Jeff in his car. He's asleep.

ANOTHER ANGLE

Onto the house. The only light now is from the spare bedroom.

INT. SPARE BEDROOM -- NIGHT

Linda, sitting up in bed reading WW DAILY (or whatever they're reading these days).

INT. MASTER BEDROOM -- NIGHT

Marvin, in bed, the snoring has stopped now.

INT. GARAGE -- NIGHT

Harry looks at his watch again. Now he figures everything must be done. He switches off the engine. He gets out of the car and untapes the hose from the tail pipe. Heads out of the garage.

EXT. GARDEN -- NIGHT

Harry goes to where the hose leads up to the bedroom, gives it a hard jerk and it comes free, making a fair amount of noise in the process.

INT. SPARE BEDROOM -- NIGHT

Linda has heard something. She gets out of bed and heads for the door.

INT. MASTER BEDROOM -- NIGHT

Linda comes in and switches on the lights.

                    LINDA
          OK hotshot! Rise and shine. I think there's
          someone creeping around outside.

Nothing from Marvin.

                    LINDA
          Marvin. Did you hear me ... wake up!

She goes over and shakes him. Nothing.

EXT. FRONT OF HOUSE -- NIGHT

Harry, carrying the hose and his carryall, comes from the back of the house and, without even seeing Jeff's car, walks off down the hill. We HOLD on the car.

ANGLE IN CAR

Jeff is sound asleep. Move in CLOSER to him and take a ...

... DISSOLVE ...

He is still asleep and over we HEAR the sound of an
ambulance. Slowly he gropes himself awake, looking out.

EXT. HOUSE -- NIGHT

The ambulance pulls into the driveway of the house. The two
guys get out and go to the front door.

ANGLE IN CAR

On Jeff. Holy shit! It's done. Linda's been murdered.

HIS POV

Now a BH police car pulls in behind the ambulance.

ANGLE IN CAR

That's it as far as Jeff's concerned. He's gotta get out
of here. He starts the engine and backs away down the
hill.

INT. MOTEL ROOM -- NIGHT

Jeff's mobile phone ringing. Patsy's hand in, groping for it.
Pull back as she answers it, showing Marilyn and the dog, all
in the same bed, sound asleep.

              PATSY
    What!

EXT. SIDE STREET - BH -- NIGHT

Jeff's car, parked. Jeff on the phone.

              JEFF
    He's done it!

       (intercut or split screen with Patsy)

              PATSY
   Who's done what?

              JEFF
   Harry. He's killed Linda.

Patsy sits up in bed, wide awake suddenly.

                    PATSY
You're kidding!

                    JEFF
The ambulance and the cops just arrived at
the house.

                    PATSY
Jesus! Poor Harry!

                    JEFF
Poor Harry, my ass. What about poor
Linda!

                    PATSY
That sounds great, coming from you.

                    JEFF
Don't get on my back right now. I can't
handle it.

                    PATSY
What are you gonna do?

                    JEFF
Emigrate. I'm an accessory to murder.

                    PATSY
Take it easy. How did he do it?

                    JEFF
How the hell should I know!

                    PATSY
Maybe he made it look like an accident.
That way you wouldn't have anything to
worry about. You've gotta find out.

                    JEFF
How'm I gonna do that?

                    PATSY
What hospital did the ambulance come from?

                    JEFF
Cedars ... I think.

                    PATSY
So get on down there.

> JEFF
> You wanna meet me there?

> PATSY
> Not much point. If he's done it, he's done
> it. Means I'm out of it. What about the guy?

> JEFF
> What guy?

> PATSY
> The guy who was banging your wife. They
> went home together didn't they ... or did
> he drop her off after dinner?

> JEFF
> Holy shit! I forgot about him ... maybe I'm
> an accessory to a double murder.

> PATSY
> You'd better get on down the hospital.

Marilyn, who's been awake for the last couple of minutes, gives
her a dig and points at the dog.

> PATSY
> Oh yeah! Marilyn wants you to pick up your
> dog soon as possible. Let me know how
> things turn out.

She hangs up. Jeff looks at his phone a beat.

> JEFF
> Thanks a bunch.

EXT. CEDARS HOSPITAL -- DAWN

An establishing shot. The night sky is beginning to lighten.

INT. NURSES STATION - HOSPITAL -- DAWN

A couple of nurses on duty behind the desk. Not much activity
in the place at this hour. Now in comes Jeff and over to the
desk.

> NURSE
> Good morning. How can I help you?

> JEFF
> My wife.

                    NURSE
Yes... ?

                    JEFF
I think she's dead.

                    NURSE
Don't you know?

                    JEFF
If I knew I wouldn't be here.

                    NURSE
Ah! She's here then, is she? Name?

                    JEFF
Tyler. Linda Tyler. She was brought in
about 20 minutes ago.

                    NURSE
No. I don't think so.

                    JEFF
I'm telling you...

He stops, looking out.

HIS POV

Linda is walking towards him, talking with a doctor.

CLOSE LINDA AND DOCTOR

                    LINDA
He never told me he had any trouble with
his heart before.

                    DOCTOR
I didn't say for sure it was a heart
attack. We'll know better when he regains
consciousness. And don't worry.

                    LINDA
Worry?

                    DOCTOR
He's going to be just fine, Mrs Tyler.

                    LINDA
Ah! Yes. Right.

By now they have reached the nurses station. There is no sign
of Jeff.

>   DOCTOR
>   I'll call you when there's any news.

>   LINDA
>   Thanks.

She starts away.

>   DOCTOR
>   He does have medical insurance, doesn't he?

>   LINDA
>   I haven't the faintest idea.

>   DOCTOR
>   I mean ... he looks the type of person
>   who'd have insurance.

>   LINDA
>   He's an attorney.

>   DOCTOR
>   That doesn't necessarily mean he'll have
>   medical insurance.

>   LINDA
>   He specialises in medical malpractice suits.

And turning, she heads out, leaving the doctor in a very
nervous state. As Linda goes, we HOLD on one of the doors
leading off the area. A moment and it opens and Jeff sticks his
head out, looking after the departed Linda. He heads over to
the station and buttonholes the doctor just as he starts back
along the passage.

>   JEFF
>   Doctor ... please. The lady you were
>   talking with just now...

>   DOCTOR
>   Mrs Tyler? What about her?

>   JEFF
>   She's OK!

>   DOCTOR
>   Yes?

                    JEFF
          I mean ... she's not a patient here?

                    DOCTOR
          No.

                    JEFF
          So who is? I mean ... who did she come in
          with?

                    DOCTOR
          Why do you want to know?

                    JEFF
          It was a man, wasn't it? Marvin Liederman.

                    DOCTOR
          An associate of yours?

                    JEFF
          Let's say we've got a lot in common. Is he
          dead?

Now the doctor's very worried.

                    DOCTOR
          Good heavens no! A minor heart attack.
          But he's going to be all right ... take my
          word for it. Truly. And he's going to be
          looked after extremely well here. We have
          state of the art equipment and the
          professional help is unmatched. Anyway,
          I'm just a house man. There's no way I can
          be held responsible.

                    JEFF
          For what?

                    DOCTOR
          For anything. I don't even have malpractice
          insurance.

Jeff looks at him for a beat. The guy's obviously overworked.

                    JEFF
          Right. Well, you take it easy, doc.

And he turns and leaves.

INT. MOTEL ROOM -- DAY

Patsy, Marilyn and the dog, still sleeping. Phone rings. Patsy
picks it up. She doesn't even ask who's calling.

                    PATSY
          OK. What now?

EXT. PARKING LOT - CEDARS -- DAY

Jeff, in his car, on the phone.

                    JEFF
          It's OK. Nobody's dead.

                    PATSY
          Great! So who was in the ambulance?

                    JEFF
          Marvin Liederman.

                    PATSY
          The lawyer who was banging your wife? I
          guess you'd call that rough justice. You
          want I should bring you something to eat
          later?

                    JEFF
          Why?

                    PATSY
          Soon as Harry finds out he fouled up, he's
          gonna try again. Back to square one. Stake
          out the house.

                    JEFF
          Maybe he won't find out. Maybe he thinks
          he's got away with it.

                    PATSY
          In which case he'll be hittin' on you for
          the money.

                    JEFF
          You're right. Fine private eye you found
          for me! He should have located Harry three
          times over by now.

                    PATSY
          Hiring a private eye was your idea.

                    JEFF
It was your friend recommended him.

                    PATSY
Do or don't you want me to bring you
breakfast?

                    JEFF
I guess. Lox, cream cheese and bagels.
Coffee without cream or sugar.

                    PATSY
        (sarcastically)
How about some fresh squeezed orange juice?

                    JEFF
Sounds good. Talk to you later.

ANGLE WIDER

Jeff drives out. Almost simultaneously, Harry's camper drives
in. Neither sees the other.

INT. HOSPITAL — NURSES STATION -- DAY

The same nurse still on duty. Harry comes in, dressed in his
mafia gear, suit, shirt, tie and fedora. He goes over to the
desk.

                    NURSE
Good morning. And how can I help you?

                    HARRY
Yeah. I'd like a copy of a death
certificate. Linda Tyler.

                    NURSE
I'm sorry...?

                    HARRY
Linda Tyler. I wanna copy of her death
certificate.

At that moment, the same doctor comes into shot delivering a
file of papers to the desk.

                    NURSE
Maybe you'd better speak to this gentleman,
doctor.

                         DOCTOR
          Yes?

                         HARRY
          Linda Tyler. I wanna copy of her death
          certificate.

                         DOCTOR
          Linda Tyler?

                         HARRY
          Jesus! How many times I gotta say it? I
          gotta have a copy of Linda Tyler's death
          certificate. I ain't got that, nobody's
          gonna believe she's dead.

                         DOCTOR
          She isn't.

                         HARRY
          Isn't what, for Christ's sake?

                         DOCTOR
          Dead.

A moment on Harry's face as it sinks in.

                         HARRY
          Ah! Thanks doc. Sorry to have bothered you.

And turning, he heads out, leaving the doctor even more
bewildered than he was before.

EXT. HOUSE -- DAY

Linda, in her designer jogging suit, setting out, followed by
Booful trotting behind her gamefully.

ANGLE

As she hits the road, she runs past a parked car. We hold on
the car. Now a head appears from beneath window level. Barney
Godwin.

ANGLE IN CAR

On Barney, as he looks after Linda. Now he picks up a sheet of
paper from the front passenger seat.

CLOSE — THE CONTRACT

"I promise to pay the bearer the sum of fifty thousand dollars as soon as my wife Linda is dead."

ANGLE ON BARNEY
He starts the engine.

ANGLE ON CAR

It takes off, up the hill, in the same direction taken by Linda. We watch it out of sight, then PAN round as Jeff's car comes up the hill. He turns off and parks, looking back at the house.

HIS POV

Everything looks OK. Linda's car is in the drive.

ANGLE — JEFF

So ... here we go again ... more watching out for Harry.

EXT. MULHOLLAND -- DAY

Linda is jogging along the side of the road along Mulholland Drive. Booful pants along behind her. Now we see Barney's car overtake her and turn the corner ahead, out of sight.

NEW ANGLE

Barney's car. He makes a U turn and stops, facing the way he's come.

ANGLE IN BARNEY'S CAR

Keeping his eye on the bend ahead where Linda will shortly appear, he dials a number on his phone.

EXT. HOUSE — ANGLE IN JEFF'S CAR

The phone rings. Jeff picks it up.

> JEFF
> Hello...

> (intercut)

> BARNEY
> This is Barney Godwin.

                    JEFF
        About time too. Where is he...?

                    BARNEY
        Who?

                    JEFF
        The guy I'm paying you to find.

                    BARNEY
        You don' have to worry about him no more.
        I'm gonna do the job m'self.

                    JEFF
        What job? What are you talking about?

                    BARNEY
        Just have the money ready. Gotta go now,
        I've got her in my sights.

Barney hangs up and looks out.

HIS POV

Linda has just turned the bend and is jogging towards CAMERA
about 200 yards away.

CLOSE BARNEY

He starts the engine.

EXT. HOUSE -- DAY. JEFF IN CAR

He's frantically stabbing out a number on his phone.

EXT. MULHOLLAND -- DAY

Barney's car ... and Linda, with Booful, jogging along the side
of the road, towards it.

CLOSE IN CAR

Barney. He checks the mirror, nothing coming from behind.
Nothing ahead.Here we go... ! He stamps on the gas.

ANGLE - WIDE

The car starts towards Linda, who's still unaware of anything
wrong.

ANGLE — CAR

As it gains speed.

CLOSE BARNEY

Behind the wheel. Really concentrating on getting it right.

CLOSE LINDA

Still unaware of her approaching doom as she jogs along.
Suddenly her phone rings. She stops dead, reaching for it in
the belt of her joggers.

ANGLE WIDE

Barney had been aiming the car for where she would have been if
she'd kept running, except now she's not there. The car mounts
the verge and goes off the side of the hill like a missile that
has just been launched.

WIDE ANGLE

The car, coming over the edge, 50 or 60 feet: down the wooded
hillside, eventually coming to a stop against a tree.

ANGLE — LINDA

Looking down, in horror. Phone still ringing. Now she pulls
herself together. She answers the phone.

> LINDA
> Sorry ... can't talk now ... gotta call an
> ambulance. Somebody just drove off the side
> of the hill.

EXT. HOUSE — ANGLE ON JEFF IN CAR

He breaks the connection with a deep sigh of relief.

EXT. HILLSIDE -- DAY

Linda looking down the hill as she dials for an ambulance.

ANGLE — BARNEY'S CAR

Smashed against a tree, smoke coming from under the hood. Now
the driver's door falls off and Barney hits the deck with just
enough reaction to show us he's not dead. He manages to roll
away from the car as it bursts into flame.

ANGLE IN CAR

The contract, on the front passenger seat, starts to burn.

EXT. RON'S HOUSE -- DAY

Re establishing. Both Ron's truck and Harry's camper are parked outside.

INT. RON'S HOUSE -- DAY

The two guys are in the kitchen eating junk from the fridge. Harry's really pissed off.

> HARRY
> I rigged her bedroom. How was I to know she wasn't gonna sleep in it? Jesus ... it's not fair.

> RON
> It was a dumb way to do it!

> HARRY
> Dumb! What dumb!

> RON
> Dumb! No personal contact. Gotta be able to see you got the right person. Like ... have the target in your sights...

Makes like firing a pistol.

> RON
> Pow! Pow!

> HARRY
> Shoot her at close range. Beat her over the head with a baseball bat. Strangle her with ma bare hands.

> RON
> (shrug)
> Stuff like that.

Long pause.

> HARRY
> I gotta tell you ... I don' think I could do that.

> RON
> Great killer you're gonna make! Yes sir, Mr
> Corleone, sure I'll knock him off for you
> ... but only if I can do it over the phone.

> HARRY
> You've talked yourself into half the money.
> You do it!

He holds out a large kitchen knife towards Ron.

> HARRY
> Here... !

Ron shakes his head in disgust.

> RON
> I never said you gotta be staring 'em in
> the eyes ... just you gotta see what's
> happenin'. Shit, the way you're goin' about
> it you could knock off half Beverly Hills
> before you get the right person.

> HARRY
> So tell me how, hot shot!

> RON
> She gotta garage up at her house?

> HARRY
> Yeah... ?

> RON
> Like with them automatic doors?

> HARRY
> I guess.

> RON
> Pool?

> HARRY
> Don't everybody in Beverly Hills got a
> pool?

> RON
> Then we're home 'n dry ... big brother.

> HARRY
> You still ain't told me how.

                         RON
          I was in the army, remember?

                         HARRY
          So?

                         RON
          So what did I do in the army?

                         HARRY
          How the fuck should I know ... you jerked
          off like the rest of 'em.

                         RON
          I was in the bomb squad. Learned me all
          'bout explosives ... boom, boom!

EXT. LINDA'S HOUSE -- DAY - ANGLE IN JEFF'S CAR

Jeff is eating the breakfast Patsy has brought him. She has
also brought him the dog, who is sitting on the floor between
his legs, grateful for every crumb Jeff feeds him.

                         PATSY
          She in there now?

                         JEFF
          Came home about half an hour ago. Cops
          dropped her off.

                         PATSY
          'n you don' know what happened.

                         JEFF
          I called a couple of hospitals. Barney Godwin's
          in Cedars. Couple of busted legs; I think.

                         PATSY
          Didn't they tell you?

                         JEFF
          All they're interested in is if he's got
          medical insurance.

                         PATSY
          Maybe Harry's given up on the whole caper
          'n gone back to Vegas. He never had much
          stayin' power.
               (thinks a moment)
          Not in any department, come to think on it.

                    JEFF
Can you find out?

                    PATSY
I can make a coupla calls. But Jeff, honey,
I gotta tell you. I don' wanna be mixed up
in this no more.

                    JEFF
Great. Just soon as we know Harry's not
gonna be trying anything.

                    PATSY
Even so. Tell the truth, I don' much care
whether Harry's in or out. I mean, I know
it's your wife who's gonna be killed 'n
all, but I got too much other stuff goin'
for me right now. More important stuff, if
you get my meaning.

                    JEFF
More important than murder!

                    PATSY
We're gonna get married.

                    JEFF
Great. But you've got to find him first.

                    PATSY
Not Harry. Me and Marilyn. She asked me
this mornin'.

                    JEFF
Congratulations ... I think.

                    PATSY
I'll be able to help her out runnin' the
motel. Maybe in a coupla years I'll get
m'self pregnant with some nice guy and
we'll have us a kid.

                    JEFF
Give me a call when you start feeling
broody. I've got good genes.

                    PATSY
Yeah! Where you been keeping 'em these past
few days?

> JEFF
> I've been under stress.

> PATSY
> You sure have. So listen. If it's OK with
> you, I'll get off here. Be on my way.

> JEFF
> You'll call Nevada first. See if he went
> home.

> PATSY
> Sure! I'll let you know.
>   (pause)
> You're a nice guy, Jeff Tyler. I hope
> everything works out for you. I mean, keep
> your fingers crossed ... maybe your wife'll
> have a fatal accident.

She leans across and gives him a kiss on the cheek. A
moment later she's out of the car and on the way down the
hill to where she's left her VW. Jeff is still looking after
her when Ron's poolman truck pulls into the driveway of the
house.

ANGLE - IN DRIVE

Ron, dressed like any other poolman, climbs out, grabs his hose
and broom and heads towards the back of the house. As far as
Jeff is concerned, he's never seen Ron before, so he doesn't
worry.

EXT. BACK OF HOUSE

Ron comes through and heads towards the pool, having a good
look around as he does so.

> LINDA
>   (voice off)
> Good morning... !

He turns like he's been shot. Linda has come out of the back
door. She is dressed smartly, obviously going out.

> RON
> Mornin' ma'am.

> LINDA
> What's happened to my regular poolman?

                    RON
          He's off sick. They asked me to take care
          of his rounds today.

                    LINDA
          I see.

A moment and she turns and heads off towards the front.

EXT. FRONT OF HOUSE -- DAY

Linda comes out. She goes down to the mailbox, checks the mail.
Something there pisses her off. She walks to her car, throws
the mail into the front seat, gets in and drives off.

ANGLE - JEFF'S CAR

Jeff starts up and drives after her. We stay on the front of
the house as Ron comes from the back, checks that Linda's gone.
Now he turns and goes back.

ANGLE - BACK OF HOUSE

Ron goes through the small door that leads into the garage.

INT. GARAGE -- DAY

Ron comes in and switches on the light. He looks around, then
he grabs a small stepladder and puts it up beneath the mecha-
nism of the garage door opener. He climbs the stepladder and,
reading from a sticker on the underside, he jots down some
numbers on a piece of paper.

EXT. BEVERLY HILLS -- DAY

Rodeo Drive possibly. Linda threads her way through the pedestrians with Booful on a leash beside her. We allow her to walk
out of shot, holding on the people for a moment before we pick
up Jeff. He too is trailing a dog, using a piece of cord as a
leash. Every now and then he jumps up to catch sight of Linda
over the heads of the pedestrians that separate them. It's hard
work, but he's doing his best. The dog, on the other hand,
isn't too happy. He'd like to take the odd sniff here and
there. This he tries to do, which forces Jeff to drag hard on
the lead every now and then. This is OK until one blue haired
MATRON interferes.

                    MATRON
          Don't do that!

> JEFF
>
> What?

> MATRON
>
> Drag on the poor dog like that. It's cruel.

Jeff can see Linda is escaping fast. He tries to move around the woman.

> JEFF
>
> Excuse me!

> MATRON
>
> Didn't you hear me, young man! You're not a fit person to have a dog.

> JEFF
>
> So you have him.

He hands the leash to the woman and makes to take off after the fast disappearing Linda. The woman shrieks.

> WOMAN
>
> Stop that man!!!

Jeff gets about five paces when he's jumped on by a couple of burly young UCLA type guys.

> YOUNG GUY
>
> OK mister! Don't you try anything smart or we'll break your face.

Jeff struggles a moment, then relaxes as he sees Linda disappear around the next corner.

> JEFF
>
> The hell with it!

EXT. LINDA'S HOUSE -- DAY

Ron's pick up is parked down the street, a hundred yards or so from the house.

ANGLE IN PICKUP

Ron and Harry. Ron has a small electrical device wired to some explosives in his hand. He's explaining it to Harry.

          RON
OK ... it's on a timer ... ten seconds
after it's activated ... boom!

          HARRY
Activated by what?

          RON
OK. How long you figure from the time she
turns into her drive there ... to reaching
the garage.

          HARRY
I dunno ... ten seconds.

          RON
You got it! Now listen to this, and tell me
I ain't one smart son of a bitch.

He holds up the home made bomb, giving it a little pat.

          RON
We fix this little beauty here so it's
waiting for her in the garage. I checked
the frequency of her door opener this a.m.
She drives up the street, see ... reaches
the driveway there and hits it ... the
opener. Soon as she done that ... the
countdown starts ... ten ... nine ...
eight. She reaches the garage doors.
They're still opening. Seven ... six ...
the doors are open now ... five, four,
three ... she drives in .... two and one
and BOOM! You're a made man and we're fifty
grand richer, the two of us.

Harry is really impressed.

          HARRY
That's somethin' else.

          RON
Ain't it just. Now all I gotta do is get in
there and put this little beauty where it's
gonna do the most good.

          HARRY
You're gonna have to wait. That's her car.

THEIR POV

Linda's car coming up the hill.

ANGLE - RON AND HARRY

Watching Linda's car. Neither have the faintest idea what's
going to happen. It's just a temporary incovenience.

ANGLE IN LINDA'S CAR.

As she turns into the drive, Linda clicks the garage opener
which is clipped to the sun visor.

ANGLE - RON AND HARRY

A small light on the bomb Ron is holding starts to blink.

> HARRY
> What's that light?

Ron looks at the bomb, then he looks out.

ANGLE - LINDA'S CAR

The garage doors are opening in front of Linda's car.

ANGLE - RON AND HARRY

Finally it hits. Ron tries to throw the bomb out of the window.
It hits the frame and falls back into the truck. He starts to
scrabble around for it between his legs. Harry's the one who
gets it. He holds it out towards Ron.

> HARRY
> Here you are ... no harm done ...

Then, even Harry twigs what's happening.

> HARRY
> Shit!!!

ANGLE - RON AND HARRY'S PICK UP

From around 25 feet away. Both doors open, but, before the guys
can jump out, the bomb goes off in the cab and they're blown
out, one in each direction, as the pick up dissolves into a sea
of flame.

EXT. HOSPITAL -- DAY

A re-establishing shot.

INT. HOSPITAL ROOM -- DAY

Ron and Harry, bandaged and splinted from head to toe, side by
side in a room. Across the room, a similarly wrapped bundle. We
don't realise it at first, but this is Barney Godwin. Jeff
comes to the door and peers in. Ron and Harry both move their
eyes in his direction (they can't move their heads). Jeff moves
to Ron's bed.

>   JEFF
>   Harry?

Ron flicks his eyes towards the next bed. Jeff moves over to
Harry.

>   JEFF
>   Harry?

Harry manages to croak a response.

>   HARRY
>   What?

>   JEFF
>   I'm Jeff Tyler.

>   HARRY
>   Listen. I quit!

>   JEFF
>   Quit?

>   HARRY
>   It ain't worth it! OK ... so you want your
>   lady dead, find some other jerk.

Jeff breathes a sigh of relief.

>   JEFF
>   Fine. I'll do that.
>   (looks around)
>   Anything you need?

A mumble from across the room. Jeff moves to the other bed,
where he recognises Barney.

                            JEFF
            Hey! Mr Godwin. How you feelin'?

                            BARNEY
            Mumble, mumble.

Jeff leans closer.

                            JEFF
            I didn't get that...

                            BARNEY
            Like shit!

                            JEFF
            Sorry about that. Incidentally, I've
            located Harry ... so you're off the
            payroll. Send me your bill soon as you're
            on your feet...
                (looks a little closer)
            ... or is that foot?

Now he turns as three porters come into the room wheeling
gurneys. They're accompanied by the doctor we've met before.

                            DOCTOR
            OK fellas ... get 'em loaded.

The porters start to load the guys onto the gurneys. He sees
Jeff.

                            DOCTOR
            Mr Tyler, isn't it...?

                            JEFF
            Hi, doc!

The doctor nods at the patients.

                            DOCTOR
            Friends of yours?

                            JEFF
            Acquaintances.

                            DOCTOR
            Not clients?

                            JEFF
            Clients?

> DOCTOR
> You told me you were into medical
> malpractice law.

> JEFF
> Not me doc. I'm a builder.

The doctor breathes a sigh of relief.

> DOCTOR
> That's a relief. I mean ... they've been
> well taken care of. Emergencies. We always
> do what we can for emergencies. But next
> time you want to visit, they'll be down at
> County Hospital. (shakes his head) No
> insurance.

We go out on a wide angle of the guys being lifted onto their
respective gurneys.

EXT. BUILDING SITE -- DAY

Start CLOSE on a sign TYLER CONSTRUCTION CO and PAN OFF to the
site. A large house is going up. A heavy duty crane is lifting
large steel girders from a flat bed truck and manoeuvring them
across the site before lowering them onto the half built house.
On site, Jeff is talking to Eddy (who we met before when he
delivered the heavy machinery to Linda's house). We are too far
away to hear what they are saying, but what we do see is Eddy
give Jeff a nudge and point out Linda's car as it turns onto
the site.

ANGLE - CLOSER

Jeff watches as Linda stops the car, gets out and, leaving the
door open, she starts towards him. She's carrying some mail and
she looks really pissed off.

> LINDA
> I want a word with you!

> EDDY
> Talk to you later, boss.

He moves away discreetly as Linda reaches Jeff and waves the
mail under his nose.

> LINDA
> Know what this is?

                        JEFF
          Looks like mail.

                        LINDA
          Your mail.

                        JEFF
          Thanks for bringing it over.

                        LINDA
          I don't want your thanks. I just want some
          of these bills paying... (riffles through
          the mail) Utilities ... my Visa card ... my
          Amex ... our account at Orbachs.

          JEFF: I never shop at Orbachs.

                        LINDA
          I do! Or I did 'til they refused to honor
          the account. God! I've never been so
          embarrassed.

                        JEFF
          I didn't think you knew how.

She looks at him a long moment.

          LINDA: Always the smartass.

She slaps the mail into his hand.

                        LINDA
          Pay them!

Turning, she starts back towards her car. Jeff looks after her,
wishing he could come up with something clever to say.

CLOSE - JEFF

A sudden metallic sound and Jeff looks up.

HIS POV - SLOW MOTION

One of the cables on the crane, swinging the steel girders, has
snapped and, even as Jeff looks up, the girder starts to fall.
Slowly, slowly.

CLOSE JEFF

He looks towards Linda.

HIS POV - SLOW MOTION

As she walks towards her car.

CLOSE JEFF

Up towards the girder once more.

HIS POV - SLOW MOTION

The girder, still falling, very, very slowly.

CLOSE - JEFF

Looking towards Linda. Will he, won't he? Shall he, shan't he?
All his troubles over in a split second. Then he makes up his
mind. He shouts a warning and runs towards her, pushing her
clear as the girder hits the ground, the end of it smashing the
hood of her car.

TWO SHOT

Close on the two of them, sprawled in the dirt , him still
clutching her. Their faces are inches apart.

                    LINDA
          You saved my life.

                    JEFF
          Can't win 'em all.

She looks at him a long moment. Shakes her head.

                    LINDA
          You're crazy.

She starts to get to her feet but slips in the mud. He grabs
at her to stop her from falling again. As he does so, there is
a yap of rage and Booful shoots out of her car, heading for
them both. He arrives and starts to chew on Jeff's ankle. But
he's hardly gotten his teeth in when there is a deep throated
woof and out of Jeff's car lumbers his dog. Booful takes one
look at it and backs off.

                    LINDA
          God, what's that?

                    JEFF
          My dog.

She straightens herself out, trying to brush off some of the
mud and dirt on her clothes.

>   LINDA
>   I should have guessed. A large, ugly
>   disagreable mutt.

>   JEFF
>   Whereas yours is a vindictive, savage,
>   extravagant little bitch.

At that moment Eddy joins them.

>   EDDY
>   You two OK?

>   JEFF
>   We're fine. Find out what happened, Eddy,
>   and make sure it doesn't happen again.

>   EDDY
>   OK, boss. Sorry 'bout this, Mrs Tyler.

Linda nods her acknowledgement. Eddy moves off. The two of them
look out towards the dogs.

ANGLE — DOGS

Booful has decided to act flirtatiously. She's prancing
around and Jeff's dog is enjoying it no end. Tails are
wagging.

>   JEFF
>   (voice over)
>   Maybe I should warn him about getting too
>   intimate. It could cost him a lot of
>   aggravation down the line.

>   LINDA
>   She can take care of herself.

JEFF AND LINDA

Watching the dogs. Now they flash each other a look. A long
moment and Linda looks towards her car. The hood has been
completely stowed in.

>   LINDA
>   What about my car?

                          JEFF
          You can tell your attorney the insurance
          will pay.

                          LINDA
          I don't have an attorney any longer.

                          JEFF
          You don't have an attorney or you don't
          have the attorney.

                          LINDA
          Neither ... but I'll be getting another.

                          JEFF
          Attorney or attorney?

                          LINDA
          A lawyer.

                          JEFF
          Ah! No doubt I'll be hearing from him.

                          LINDA
          No doubt at all.
             (changes subject)
          But right now my problem is getting home.

                          JEFF
          I'll drive you.

                          LINDA
          Thank you...

She turns towards the dogs.

                          LINDA
          Come on Booful.

ANGLE — DOGS

Real friendly now. A whole lot of sniffing going on.
Reluctantly, it seems, Booful turns and trots towards Linda.
Jeff's dog follows eagerly.

ANGLE — WIDE

Jeff and Linda, followed by the dogs, heading for Jeff's car.

                    LINDA
          Giving me a ride doesn't entitle you to any
          privileges.

                    JEFF
          I didn't think it would.

                    LINDA
          One drink ... that's all you're gonna get.

                    JEFF
          Out of my wine cellar.

                    LINDA
          I'll pour it from my fifty per cent.

They reach the car. The two dogs jump into the back. Jeff gets
into the driver's side while Linda tries to do the same on the
passenger side. The door is locked.

ANGLE IN CAR

Jeff leans across to unlock the door. As Linda opens it to
get in, he spots a piece of paper on the floor. He picks it
up, glancing at it. Shit! It's the contract. He screws it
up quickly and drops it out of the window. Now he starts
the car.

                    JEFF
          I've been thinking about this fifty per
          cent bullshit. What if I decided to spend
          the lot? Fifty per cent of nothing is
          nothing.

                    LINDA
          If you're going to spend it, I'm going to
          do my share.

The car starts away. We let it go, holding its departure as it
turns from the site onto the highway.

                    JEFF
             (voice over)
          I figured you'd say that.

                    LINDA
             (voice over)
          So don't go taking any trips without me.

                    JEFF
               (voice over)
          Where do you want to go?

                    LINDA
               (voice over)
          I'd really like a visit to New York.

                    JEFF
               (voice over)
          I hate New York.

                    LINDA
               (voice over)
          So stay home and mind the dogs.

The car is now practically out of sight. Then into foreground
steps Eddy, looking after the car. He shakes his head. He is
about to move off when he bends down and picks up the screwed
up contract Jeff threw from the car. He straightens it out,
reads it, looks out to where the car has disappeared, back to
the contract. Then he folds the contract carefully and tucks it
into his pocket. Around here, we...

... FADE OUT

                    THE END

Three

Dialogue and character

You've read *Fifty Fifty* and hopefully liked it enough to carry on with this book. Actually, 'liked' is the wrong word. You're not required to 'like' it. For all I know, you might hate that kind of movie. But that wasn't the object of the exercise.

I originally intended to write a chapter on dialogue and another on character but the two are so interdependent it's probably best to deal with them at the same time. Award-winning director Mike Leigh won't even think about one without the other. He establishes with his actors the characters he wants them to assume, then he gets them to make up the dialogue as they go along, making up the story at the same time. Great for Mike Leigh, but not much need of a screenwriter.

OK! So what did I want to write? A drama or a comedy? I was a little bored with dramas. I'd written six or seven of them. So let's try a comedy... First, what's your story? Where does it come from? My advice up front is try to stick to stuff you know about. In the case of *Fifty Fifty*, it came partially from personal experience. And before you go calling the law with information about a guy who might or might not kill his soon-to-be ex-wife, let me enlarge on that a little. I *did* get a divorce in California and, after some arguments between lawyers, I *did* sign over 50 per cent of our assets, including the house in Beverly Hills. As far as I was concerned, end of story. Move on.

But what if I'd been one of those guys like Jeff who, to drown his sorrows, gets fall-down drunk and basically wishes out loud that his wife was dead? And what if he, without being aware of it, tells some guy what he's feeling and the guy he tells is a crazy like Harry? So, realising what he's done, he tries to cancel the contract. And there it is. So block out the rough progression you're after, bearing in mind your three-act structure, and see if it works.

OK, so you've got your storyline, your plot – beginning, middle and end – roughly broken down into three acts. This automatically means that you have an outline idea of your principal characters, your hero and your villain. Perhaps I shouldn't refer to the villain as a person. It could be a robot or an impending volcano, a typhoon or, in the case of my movie *X the Unknown*, a monster from the centre of the earth. But assuming he or she is a person as opposed to a thing, you have to let the reader know what *kind* of a person as quickly as possible.

I was listening to somebody give a lecture the other day, the head of drama for a TV production company with a string of successes behind them. She said that, as far as she is concerned, a piece can run for 50 minutes before you actually start the story, as long as that 50 minutes is being used to establish character. She's a bright lady, no doubt about that, and she's had some pretty good shows on the air. But 50 minutes before starting the story? I'm afraid I can't see it. Five minutes, maybe. And, even then, try to get an inkling of the storyline introduced. Because you can't hang around too long introducing a lot of characters in a vacuum. You have to let your audience know the milieu you are placing them in and the only way to do that, in my opinion, is get the story going. You can't spend three quarters of an hour developing a character without giving some indication of what he is about, what he's involved in.

There are two ways of introducing the main character up front. First, you can physically describe him as I have done in *Fifty Fifty* (page 23).

```
Linda is an attractive, rangy-looking woman. A two-year-old
face-lift gives her a slight wind-tunnel look. She's also, in
her time, had a tummy tuck, breast implant and liposuction.
She is around 40 but would never admit to being more than 35
and then only under extreme pressure. She can be sexy,
provocative and charming but her natural inclinations are
predatory. She makes no moves, takes no decisions without
first asking the question "What's in it for Linda?" She works
on and off as a Beverly Hills real estate salesperson. She is
bonded to a vicious little poodle named Booful.
```

As far as I'm concerned, that paints a pretty good picture of the person, not only physically but, to some extent, characterwise too. While some of the screenwriting textbooks deplore the use of actor's names, if you really want to visually tie your character right down you could always start the paragraph...

```
Linda is an attractive, rangy-looking woman (think Michelle
Pfeiffer or Sigourney Weaver) ...
```

This isn't to suggest that you might get either of these ladies for the part (you should be so lucky) but it gives the reader an immediate physical picture of the character he/she is reading about. In the description of JEFF TYLER which follows, you could add (think Billy Crystal) ...

But read page twenty-three again, the two characters. Even without the Michelle Pfeiffer or Billy Crystal references, one should have a pretty good idea of who and what they are.

Also on the first page in the script, we've established the location, which gives the reader a general idea of the social area we're dealing with, namely middle-class Beverly Hills. The dialogue in the opening scene sets the style and points to the direction the storyline is going to take.

The next scene (page 27) between MARTY and JEFF steers the storyline onto its next stage, namely that JEFF believes he's in deep shit and LINDA is going to take him for a ride. What the hell is he going to do about it?

He gets spiteful is what he does (page 30). Completely impractical, but the kind of thing that a character like JEFF would do. A kind of "I'll show you, bitch!" And to crown it all, he slugs his wife's lawyer then slugs a cop into the bargain. And his reaction? He's going out to get fall-down drunk.

So, by page 30, we have established exactly the type of guy JEFF is, together with the fact that we don't know what the hell he's going to do about the situation he's in. All this we've done with dialogue. We haven't actually *seen* anything happen, apart from his directing the building equipment into the driveway. We didn't *need* to see the arrival of Linda's lawyer, him getting slugged followed by the cop. In this case, the whole thing is more effectively delivered in JEFF's one small speach.

```
                    JEFF
        I slugged the creep who's fucking my wife.
        I just kinda pushed one of the cops who
        tried to stop me.
```

And knowing JEFF as we already do, we can see the whole scene as it must have taken place. Maybe there'll be a director who'll want to shoot that scene, especially as it's not in the script. It'll be one of his ways of establishing his creative rights. The fact that it'll probably be left on the cutting-room floor won't bother him. He'll insist that it goes in on the first or 21st rewrite. Dealing with that is another matter which we'll take care of later.

The next scene, in the bar with STEVE, is purely a set-up scene to deliver JEFF to where we want him to end up, namely a lowlife joint in Nevada where we meet the two main subsidiary characters, PATSY and HARRY. So as a running character, STEVE doesn't concern us all that much. We use him and we lose him.

We follow on with the scenes where the main drive of the story is laid out and we develop further PATSY's character. She comes over as a tough lady who's seen it all and knows how to take care of herself.

Act One ends on page 42 as they set out to try solve the problem that JEFF has created for himself. So, in Act One we have established the main characters, established the plot line and set Act Two in motion.

Act Two starts with HARRY, establishing his target. JEFF continues to bumble around like a spare prick at a wedding, not sure what the hell he's going to do about the situation he's got himself into. We also have a sequence between JEFF and LINDA where, for one brief moment, things seem to warm up between them (page 48). This is a small precursor of the last scene in the script. It also provides the faintest hint that maybe things between them are not completely over.

Next we meet RON, Harry's brother, who finds and copies the 'contract'. HARRY turns up and agrees to accept RON as a fifty-fifty partner, which points to the fact that the money isn't what HARRY is really after. This is confirmed in the next scene where he meets up with the Italian restaurant owner, LUIGI.

Meanwhile, following JEFF, we meet the private eye BARNEY, who a little later finds the 'contract'. HARRY tries his first hit on LINDA and gets her boyfriend MARVIN instead. End Act Two.

Act Three deals with the second murder attempt and the way it goes wrong, with everyone getting their just desserts. We end the movie with the scene between JEFF and LINDA where it really looks as if they might get together again, with the kick of EDDY finding the contract.

I've tried, in this short chapter, to get over to you some ideas about the developing of characters with dialogue. OK, so we use the situations as well, the plot-line, if you like, but 85 per cent is in the dialogue. For example, there's Jeff's lawyer MARVIN, who thinks tennis is far more important than what Jeff is going through. Then there's RON, Harry's brother. He's defined almost immediately as slightly simple-minded, when he comes out dressed as a cowboy because he's going to clean a director's pool and he hopes he'll get cast in an upcoming movie.

```
                    RON
      Matter of fact ahmm an actor, but parts are
      difficult to come by right now. A guy's
      gotta be on the ball. Today ahm doing this
      director's pool. Variety says he's casting
      a new Western movie 'n' I figure if he's at
      home and he looks out of his window while
      ahm there, ahm a dead cert to get a part.
      Might even get a speakin' part. It's all
      there is, that one speech.
```

Then we get the private eye, BARNEY. Before we even meet him, we know he's a loser because he's scared of the fact that his visitor might be a cop. All this is confirmed later in the scene as we realise the only work he can get is looking for lost animals. But Jeff hires him anyway.

And having just explained at great length the importance of dialogue, another piece of advice, also to do with dialogue, is always to bear in mind that you are writing a motion picture. Think about that for a moment, a 'motion picture'. If a situation is more effective expressed in dialogue, then so be it. But if you can do it equally well with moving pictures, then do it that way. *Fifty Fifty* is designed as a comedy, so there is more dialogue in it than there would be if it were a thriller. You could use the same basic characters, and virtually the same storyline, and come up with a completely different movie. A man takes out a contract on his wife then changes his mind and tries to cancel the contract. The character of Harry is in it for the money and he won't *allow* Jeff to pull out. In other words, a movie in the genre of *Double Indemnity* or *Strangers on a Train*. Movies that allow for more action and less dialogue. In fact, it sounds like a good idea. Maybe I'll rewrite *Fifty Fifty* and this time I'll sell it.

One final word about dialogue. It's going to be changed. First by you, then by everybody else who gets the chance. Producer, director, actor, they'll all want changes. Unless you're a Harold Pinter or a David Mamet the words are definitely *not* sacred. And it's no good yelling and screaming about it. Apart from the fact that you're not going to be around anyway (writers never are), in my opinion the people who are involved in the actual shooting of your script, the ones who invested money in the project, are entitled to do whatever they want with it. They bought it from you and they now own it. And if they think they have a better chance of selling the end product by changing dialogue or, for that matter, anything else they don't like, then so be it. Right or wrong, let them make the changes. With any luck you'll be far too busy on your next project to give a damn one way or the other.

Four

Treatments and rewrites

After the storyline comes the treatment. It's at this stage that the characters are fleshed out and the story developed. Some writers deliver treatments of 25 pages or less. Me... I do most of the work in the treatment. Around 65 pages. Virtually the script without the dialogue. But that's just the way I work. There are no set rules.

There's very little point in writing a full screenplay if the treatment isn't right and acceptable, just as there's no point in writing a treatment until the storyline is tied down. So, wherever possible, have your intended buyer come aboard as soon as possible. After the pitch has been accepted, do the storyline. The genre of the subject will have been established already. So aim for two pages maximum. Block out the central characters, describe their goal, then hint at the difficulties they are going to encounter achieving it.

Take *Fifty Fifty* for an example. Jeff Tyler, a middle-aged guy with a roving eye, who runs a successful Beverly Hills construction outfit, is splitting up with his wife Linda, who's having an affair with her attorney. His lawyer tells him that a divorce is going to cost him 50 per cent of everything he owns. Horrified, he gets fall-down drunk and eventually passes out. When he recovers the next morning, a bar waitress, Patsy, tells him that he has offered her sometime boyfriend Harry, a slightly simple-minded bartender, $50,000 to kill Linda. Now, assisted by Patsy, Jeff must find Harry and cancel the deal, at the same time not letting Linda know what he has set in motion.

Harry's first try at killing Linda goes wrong, sending Linda's current lawyer/boyfriend to hospital. So, for his second attempt, he enlists the aid of his equally simple-minded brother Ron, a Beverly Hills pool cleaner. This too turns out catastrophically, sending the two brothers to hospital, where Jeff eventually confronts Ron and cancels the contract. Finally there is a chance that Jeff and Linda might get together again... with one small snag.

OK, that's it. The Storyline. And having got that accepted, one moves on to the treatment. But, let's face it, nobody's going to come up with a straight storyline like that unless they've worked out a hell of a lot of the detail about the direction the treatment and, eventually, the screenplay is going to take. And here's the chance to get it down on paper.

The treatment can run any length that suits. Its purpose is to give the reader an overall view of the project. We already know the storyline, now we start to build the characters. As I have said earlier, I do most of my work at this stage, almost a script without the dialogue unless there is a line of dialogue which tells the reader something succinct about the plot or the character which otherwise might take a couple of sentences to describe. For example, in *Fifty Fifty*:

```
                    JEFF
          I slugged that creep who was fucking my
          wife. I just kinda pushed one of the cops
          who tried to stop me. Shit, I hardly
          touched him.
```

Try describing this scene, which we never actually shoot in the script, using description rather than dialogue. Apart from taking up at least a page, it's irrelevant because it is the consequences of the scene rather that the scene itself that are important.

One last word on treatments. Never dive into a script until you've got your treatment written, rewritten, and then written again. Try to get the potential buyer involved at this stage. If you *have* got somebody interested in the project, and assuming they have agreed on the storyline, they might put their hands in their pockets for the treatment. It's not likely, but it's worth a try.

Let's talk about rewrites. You're going to be doing a lot of them.

Rewriting has become such an occupational hazard that columnist Dave NcNary wrote a long piece on it in *Variety* not long ago. His first sentence – "Screenwriters are freaking at Hollywood's endless tweaking" – is typical *Variety* headlining, but, as with all their columns and features, it hits the nail right on the head. Go buy yourself *Variety* every now and then, the international edition. It's full of trade talk, grosses, reviews both for movies and TV and, as with this article by Dave McNary, it's also full of very readable material relative to what we are trying to do here. Unfortunately, the tweaking he refers to isn't confined to Hollywood. Just as much goes on in the UK. Probably in France too. Certainly in Germany, a market of which I have had personal experience. But we'll get to that end of the subject later and deal with rewrites from the start.

You finish your first draft and you type my four favourite words.

```
FADE OUT.

                    THE END
```

Wonderful feeling. Talk about euphoria. There it is, all 120 pages. Blood, toil, tears and sweat. So what next? Somebody has got to read it. And the best person to give it the first going-over is yourself. Stick it in a drawer for a couple of days, go out, get drunk, go to the movies, whatever, but try to forget about it. Then, brace yourself, dig it out of the drawer and read it.

"Maybe if I change that scene around a bit..."

"The lead character's got no background..."

"Perhaps I should move that sequence back a couple of pages..."

"The dialogue isn't too hot in the final scene..."

It's almost a dead cert you're going to spot holes in what you've written and you're going to want to put them right. So, back to the computer and start cutting and pasting and rethinking. But the trouble with self-imposed rewrites is knowing when to stop, knowing when things are just becoming different rather than better. Somewhere along the line you have to say "This is it. This is as good as it's going to get. End of rewrites." Let's get the thing off in the mail to all those people out there, one of whom is going to pay you a vast sum of money and make you famous.

So, having made *your* changes, move on to the next stage. Somebody else to read it. A nearest and dearest? Not a good idea if they're not in the business. Scripts aren't easy to read if you're not used to it. So, maybe a friend in the film and/or writing trade. Somebody who will give you a straight and honest opinion. Dream on!

If, although it's unlikely at this stage, you have an agent, then he's the guy/gal to give it to. After all, he/she is the one who's going to have to try sell it. But whatever... *somebody's* got to read it and make a few suggestions.

Some of these suggestions you might go along with, mostly you won't. And so the rewrites begin.

Finally comes a time when you say (again) enough is enough. End of rewrites until you get somebody interested enough in the project to put their hands in their pockets...

"Somebody interested" covers any number of people. At the top you have a studio or production company, at the bottom you have the guy who claims to be a good friend of Spielberg and would like to run with your project. He can't afford to give you any money up front, but if you do a couple of rewrites, which he's more than willing to help you with, he's sure to get the property to the man himself. Whereas the studio or production company say sure they're interested, providing you'll change this and alter that. Only then, if they like the rewrites, will they discuss coming up with any money. And we writers go along with this crap because it's the only way forward that we can see.

In the old days, long gone now, if a company was interested in a property they'd make a deal for a first draft, two sets of revisions and a polish. Money would be agreed on and paid on delivery of the various segments. Nowadays the powers that be demand a limitless number of rewrites before they'll even discuss putting their hands in their pockets. And, let's face it, there's nothing you can do about it. Sure, you can tell them you're not going to do any more rewrites unless you get paid, so they go to some other poor schmuck who'll take over your work and try to make as many changes as possible so he'll be entitled to a credit on the end product.

But unfortunately, rewriting is part of the lifeblood of script development. And it goes on far into the production schedule. During shooting, script changes are made on a daily basis for any number of reasons: the weather on location; the director doesn't think this particular actor can say that particular line; the actor doesn't *want* to say this and the actress doesn't *want* to say that or they can't say it or they bloody well *won't* say it; the producer wants to move a scene from here to there because he decides he can't afford to build another set...

All this goes on and you, as the original writer, know nothing about it because you're long gone and forgotten. Maybe, a year down the line you'll see the movie advertised and maybe, just maybe, your name will be there along with a couple of people you've never heard of who share screen credit as writers. Checking back through my credit list, I see I shared screenplay credit on almost a dozen occasions.

SCREENPLAY BY JIMMY SANGSTER AND CHARLIE FARNSBARNES.

This conjures up a vision of a couple of guys sitting around, batting out a story, trying out the dialogue on each other and generally working together. This may be true in some cases. Billy Wilder & I A L Diamond who, among other movies, wrote *Some Like It Hot* and *Irma La Douce*, or, for UK television, Frank Muir & Denis Norden. But in the vast majority of cases multiple titles are an indication of multiple rewrites, each one sufficient to earn the author a screen credit and, down the line, residual payments. So, ask me the question, "What was Charlie Farnsbarnes like to work with?" and my answer is, I haven't the faintest idea, I never met him. Naturally the same thing applies in reverse. Charlie Farnsbarnes wrote a script and somewhere down the line it was handed to Jimmy Sangster to do a rewrite.

The first time it happened to me was on a script I wrote called *The Concrete Jungle*. (They later changed the title to *The Criminal*.) It was an original screenplay and I rather liked it. It was early in my writing career and I wasn't aware of the pitfalls one could encounter. The producer eventually signed the late, great Joe Losey to direct the movie. Only problem was, while Losey liked the basic script, he insisted on rewrites. Not only that, he had his favourite writer do them. The first I knew of all this was when I saw an ad for the movie with the credit:

SCREENPLAY BY ALUN OWEN
FROM A STORY BY JIMMY SANGSTER

I threw a real wobbly. I called the producer in a high old state of dudgeon. "How dare they?" "Never been treated so badly!" Stuff like that. Eventually, in a fit of pique I told them to take my name off the film altogether. Which was stupid of me because it went on to win some kind of a prize at the Edinburgh Festival. I like to think it was because of the story, but even I have to admit it was a pretty good movie. But to this day I think I was screwed over the credit. I'm sure Alun Owen won't agree and Joe Losey's dead so he can't vote one way or the other. So what's the point of bitching about it any more? – except to use it as an example of what can happen to you in the rewrite jungle.

The Writer's Guild of America provides the writer with some kind of protection from all this. Article 18 of the Writer's Guild Basic Agreement requires that, at the time a writer is assigned to a project, the Company must notify the writer of the names of all other writers then working on the project, all other writers who have previously written on the project, and/or all writers from whom literary material has been acquired on which the writer is employed. The Guild goes on to emphasise the value of this information. At the beginning of a project, writers should know if prior material exists which will affect their credit, their rights and/or their creative contribution.

Basically, these rules provide that the writers should never be surprised by the intended screen credits when the movie is finished and released. While, as the Guild points out, this can affect the writer's self-esteem, there is also a practical element inasmuch as they affect residuals, creative rights, etc.

Another function provided by the WGA is their title arbitration system. If there is any dispute about who wrote what and how the credits should read, the whole mess is turned over to the WGA. They get hold of all the material from the original storyline, through the treatment, first, second, third draft screenplays etc, remove everybody's names from the title pages and then send the whole lot out to half a dozen writers who read everything and decide what they think the final credits should be. They submit their ideas to an arbitrator who goes with the majority. Screenplay by A and B from a story by C. And whatever these writers decide, that's it. No more arguing.

I was involved in this process many times, from both sides of the fence. There's an awful lot of rewriting goes on and many times I would be hired to do a rewrite on something and the original creator wouldn't accept that I'd done enough work to deserve a credit so the whole thing would go to arbitration. Sometimes I won, sometimes I lost. But it is a fair system, and you can't argue with it.

A piece of good advice. If you can, try to get paid for doing a major rewrite. Get something down on paper. When I was in Los Angeles I wrote an original script for a real big-time production executive. I went the normal route: sold him the story idea, next stage the treatment, then the first draft screenplay and finally a set of rewrites. Got paid my money per contract and moved to pastures new. Then two producers come aboard and please can they have some more rewrites. But, unfortunately, they didn't have any more money. We have a meeting and, seeing the changes they wanted weren't too drastic, I said I'd do them in exchange for two first class round-trip airplane tickets Los Angeles/London. They agreed. I did the rewrites. They said they didn't like them and I could whistle for my tickets. I called the WGA and they told me I'd been conned and there was nothing they could do about it.

I saw the movie they eventually made. It had very little to do with my original script, but my name was up there with two other writers, so I *did* come in for some residuals. One small consolation was that the *Motion Picture Guide* said the movie was "...dry, dull, and terribly predictable." They should have gone with my script!

Something similar happened on the next movie I did in LA. Only this time they didn't even ask me to do rewrites, they just went out and hired two other guys. But again I shared a credit. John Huston directed the movie, *Phobia*, and again the *Motion Picture Guide* gave their verdict: "...a simple minded script that will leave most viewers bored after the first fifteen minutes." I'd like to be able to say they'd have done better going with my original but, in this particular case, I don't think they would.

So be prepared to spend as much or more time doing rewrites than you spent on the original. Treat each rewrite session as if you were doing an adaptation (next chapter), which, in fact, it is. Whether you are rewriting your own material or somebody else's, the groundwork has been done and you are 'adapting' the material to fit whatever parameters have been set. Your hands are tied somewhat by the fact that the people/guy/corporation who bought and paid for the script in the first place obviously saw something in it they liked. So ask yourself, why do they want changes?

Maybe they bought the script because they liked the basic idea/storyline and now they want a complete rewrite. Perhaps they've just taken a director on board who wants the changes or maybe they want the changes to attract a star actor/actress. Perhaps they have the star lined up already and he/she has insisted on these changes. It would be a great help if you, the writer, were aware of what the people are looking for in their rewrite. Then try to give it to them, because if you don't, they'll go out and hire someone else.

Somebody once said that scripts are not written, they're rewritten. I'm not sure who it was, but he sure as hell knew what he was talking about.

Five

Television

 few years back, writing for TV was pretty much the same as writing for the movies. That was especially the case in America, where, at different times, I worked as a writer, a script editor and a producer of network TV shows.

The whole thing started by accident. I was in Los Angeles doing a rewrite on a movie I'd written in England for an American company. I finished the job, packed my suitcase and booked my ticket home, when I got a call from Hammer in London saying that Screen Gems, the TV branch of Columbia, were calling from LA trying to locate me. I called my LA agent and told him to check it out. He called back to tell me that Screen Gems had just sold a series idea to a network and were looking for me to see if I'd like to come aboard as a story consultant.

The only TV I'd done was a couple of *Armchair Theatres*, episode one of *The Saint* (which was completely rewritten by the American script editor when he came aboard), and two four-part serials. All this had been early in my career, when TV shows were transmitted live. Being a serial, the episodes were supposed to finish with a cliffhanger to make sure everyone tuned in next week. The first episode of the first one I wrote over-ran, so the cliffhanger never got onto the screen. So episode two started with our hero escaping from a situation nobody had seen him get into. About then I decided I didn't want to work for television any more. Apart from anything else, the money was terrible. I'd stick to movies. Something I did for the next six or seven years.

So, because I hadn't been involved with TV, I didn't even know what a story consultant did. My agent assured me it was an important job, one step down from series producer, and the money was good.

"But what does he do?" I wanted to know.

"Don't worry about it," said my agent. "They're lucky to get you. I had to do a big selling job."

"I thought they called me,"

"It was still a hard sell."

Even if someone is begging for you on bended knees, your agent will invariably tell you "It was a hard sell."

The deal was for 13 weeks with options at the end exercisable by either party... which meant that, at the end of 13 weeks, I could quit or they could fire me. In fact, they picked up the option and I was there for nearly a year. By then, any ideas I had of returning to England were long gone. I had a new wife, a large mortgage on a Beverly Hills house, three cars in the garage and, most important of all, I was having a ball.

As to why me they wanted me, there were a couple of reasons. One, the producer, Bill Castle, had met me when making a film for Hammer a few years before and, two, this upcoming series was entitled *Ghost Story* and I had the reputation of being able to write scary stuff.

So, with a certain amount of trepidation, and a promise that I could direct at least two of the episodes, I took the job. After a great deal of trial and error, I worked out what the story consultant was supposed to do. Basically, I would take meetings with writers whom I thought capable of turning out a good script for the series. These were usually writers the consultant had worked with before, which left me a bit high and dry because I was a new boy in town. But my agent took care of that. The day I started there was a note from him listing half a dozen names. Who are these guys, I wanted to know. He told me they were writers who he personally recommended would do a good job for me. "Also they're clients of mine and some of them could do with the money."

So, stage one of being a story consultant is you call in a writer, tell him roughly what the series is about, maybe invite him to a screening of the pilot and then you ask him if he can come up with a story idea which fits the series concept. If and when he does, you run it past the producer, who either buys the idea or not. Assuming he does, the writer goes off and, in stages, delivers a storyline, a treatment and finally a shooting script. If, on the other hand, the writer can't come up with an idea, the story consultant and the producer might give him one to work with because this is a writer they want to use. You know he's going to keep the script within the parameters laid down by the series concept.

The second show on which I worked as a story consultant was called *Movin' On*. It was the adventures of a couple of truck drivers down South. Each week they'd drive into another town, Memphis, New Orleans, you name it, where they would get involved with some local problem, sort it out and move on. Unfortunately, out of all the writers we interviewed, only about three came up with usable storylines, so Ernie Frankel, the producer, and I drafted out around 20 more. Then we commissioned various writers to work on them.

Some were OK, most weren't. I got so tired of rewriting scripts from page one and then typing in the original writer's name on the credit list, I said the hell with it and typed my own name. I'd come up with the story and now I'd rewritten the script. I felt I was entitled. Not once did anyone object, as they were entitled to. The Writer's Guild have special arbitrations to deal with such matters and if any writer feels they're entitled to a credit, shared or otherwise, the Guild will eventually rule on it.

One of the first things I learned about TV writing was that writing for a one-hour episodic series was the same as writing a short movie. As far as construction is concerned, the piece *has* to conform to the three-act structure to accomodate the commercials and, in the case of *Ghost Story* – which was a show without a running character, every week was a completely new deal – character development was similar too. And, let's face it, dialogue is dialogue and, as I've said elsewhere, everyone is going to have a go at changing that.

Added to this was the fact that I didn't have to write the bloody things anyway. The producer and I would work out a basic storyline then call in a writer we could trust, give him the storyline and send him off to write the script. He would deliver a treatment which we'd mess around with, give him notes and he'd go off and write a first draft. We'd mess with that too – sometimes, as I've just mentioned, rewriting from page one. Sometimes the network would want to see a script before it was shot, but not often. Then, finally, we'd shoot the thing. Fifty minutes screentime to be shot, on location, in six days. If I thought I had problems getting the script right, think of the poor director.

Back then, apart from the daytime soaps, practically all TV shows were either half-hour comedy shows or episodic one-hour shows, each one a complete story, although, unlike *Ghost Story*, they were centred around a running character or characters, be it *Columbo* or *Mission: Impossible* in America or *The Saint* or *Doctor Who* in the UK. And in both cases the set-up was the same. A producer and a script editor employed outside writers to pen an episode, which they would then fiddle with and finally shoot. The main difference was that in the UK the broadcasters would order half a dozen episodes, in the US they'd order 22.

Now, unfortunately, it's different. Eighty five per cent of TV drama is written by a group of writers on staff. The other 15 per cent is written by poor schmucks like you and me who manage to get an introduction to someone who is running a show, who tells them to write a trial script, "just to see we all know what we're dealing with." The trial script is written and delivered. It is then screwed about and a second draft is asked for. Then a third. Finally, if you're very lucky, some of it will be incorporated into the show and your name will appear along with eight or nine other writers who happen to be on staff.

So how do you get on staff? Or, more specifically, how do you get to be on the staff of an American show because, let's face it, that's what everyone wants. That's where the money and the kudos is. First, you've got to be living in Los Angeles and there you write a spec script for a show that's already on the air, one that you know well and would like to be associated with. If you can get your dummy run to the guy who runs the show, he'll read it to find out if you know what you're doing. To do this it's almost mandatory that you have an agent. The same rule applies to TV as to movies, stuff doesn't get read unless it comes through an agent. So, the head guy reads it and decides whether or not you understand the characters and the basic situation and, while he's about it, whether you know how to write. Then, and only then, you might get yourself a meeting, first with the head guy, then maybe with the rest of the team.

Next time you watch an American TV show, count the number of writer's credits. They'll appear as executive producers, producers, co-producers, story consultants, even as writers, but take my word for it, they're *all* writers. Watching a half-hour comedy show the other night (which shall be nameless), I counted eleven. Pretty impressive, I thought. Then I read an article in the *Observer* by Mark Levine, who was writing about the upcoming demise of *Friends*, in which he said *their* staff of writers ran to 13, eight men and five women all under 30 years old, of whom a good few are credited as being executive producers. This is not confined to TV. There are plenty of theatrical movies which credit four or five writers.

But there are areas of UK TV which are completely the opposite, with sitcoms being written by one or two writers. *Coupling* has one writer, Steven Moffat, while his wife, Sue Vertue, produces. Apparantly, the format has been bought by US TV as a replacement for *Friends*, which is drawing to a close. Then there is *The Office*, another hugely succesful BBC show which has two guys, Stephen Merchant and Ricky Gervais, who write and direct all the shows. And going back through the classic sitcoms on UK TV – shows like *Steptoe & Son, Porridge, Dad's Army* – they were all penned by one or two writers. But as I have mentioned elsewhere, these shows tend to appear in batches of six, whereas the US sitcoms are made in batches of 22 or more.

But, somewhere down the line, be it 22 episodes or 122, the show had to be created. Somebody wrote the original pilot episode. He didn't have six writers on staff. Like you, he probably worked at home, sweating over every page, wondering if the bloody thing was ever going to earn him any money. Try it. I did. I wrote the following especially for this book.

Designed to be shot in the UK, it could easily transfer to America. As for how I came up with the piece in the first place, it's difficult to pin down. I wanted a light-hearted story with a couple of strong characters. By strong I don't mean powerful, I mean well-defined. I was watching a girl in a restaurant one evening. She was with a guy who was chatting her up and while she was half-listening to him, I could see that her mind was somewhere else. Like I said, she was half-listening, nodding her head from time to time, but she was in another world. I thought about it later. Where was she? What was going on? What was she dreaming about? And there was the basic story idea. As for formulating the character, I went the *Bridget Jones* route.

Maybe somewhere down the line I might try to sell it. But only to a UK buyer. The thought of sitting around a table with half a dozen other writers sweating out the next 15 episodes? Forget it!

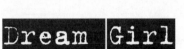

A comedy series
created and written by
Jimmy Sangster

PRINCIPAL CHARACTERS

KATE
29 years old. Middle-class upbringing. Pretty and bright. Given
to day-dreaming occasionally. A true romantic, slightly
dreading her upcoming 30th birthday. She runs her own business,
Kate's Pantry, a small catering service which does board room
lunches and/or private dinner parties.

JOANNA
She's a couple of years older than Kate, an American, living in
London. She's Kate's partner and flat mate. She's more of a
realist than Kate, more cynical.

EDWARD
Edward Barton Smith QC. Sixty years old, elegant, charming and
attractive.

MARY
Edward's ex-wife. Around 55 years old. Smart, good-looking,
sophisticated and intimidating.

There will be other characters appearing in later episodes,
including the two grown-up children of Edward and Mary.

DREAM GIRL

FADE IN...

EXT. CITY OFFICE BUILDING -- DAY

An establishing shot. A small van parked out front with the
sign KATE'S PANTRY stencilled on the side.

INT. BOARD DINING ROOM -- DAY

KATE is just checking the last of the place settings, probably
half a dozen. Now she turns and goes through a door...

INT. BOARD ROOM KITCHEN -- DAY

...into the kitchen. Where she checks on the food she's already
laid out and the containers heating in the cooker. Now she
checks her watch.

                KATE
    Oh God!

Goes to the wallphone and punches out a number.

                KATE
    Oh God! Oh God!

She gets through.

                KATE
    Reception? OK. This is Kate Norman, Kate's
    pantry. I'm doing a lunch in the boardroom
    upstairs. Listen, I'm expecting a waiter.
    Has anyone been asking for me down there?
    No... all right.
        (hangs up)
    Oh God! I'm going to have to serve the meal
    myself... and cook it... and wash it up...
    oh God!

                VOICE OFF
    Excuse me!

She turns. A man, EDWARD, has his head stuck round the door.

                EDWARD
    Is this the boardroom?

A look of relief on Kate's face, immediately replaced by anger.

                KATE
    About bloody time too... !

INT. OFFICE -- DAY

This is the office of Kate's Pantry. A converted mews house. In
this, the main room on the ground floor, there are the kitchen
stoves, fridges etc, together with a small desk with a
computer. There is a staircase leading up to the apartment
above where the two girls live.

                KATE
    How was I to know he was the guest of

honour? I mean... he was half an hour
early.

Kate and JOANNA, discussing the lunch. Kate is seated at the
desk looking over some mail, mostly bills.

> KATE
> Oh... great! The bank says that unless we
> can come up with ten thousand pounds within
> the next seven days... that's it. Finish.
> Kaput. End of Kate's Pantry.

> JOANNA
> So who was he?

> KATE
> Who?

> JOANNA
> The guest of honour.

> KATE
> Oh! One of the top QCs in the country.
> That's what mein host, the client told me...
> when he'd calmed down.

> JOANNA
> What's a QC?

> KATE
> A Queen's Council.

> JOANNA
> Does that make him royal?

> KATE
> He's a lawyer. I mean... it's no big deal.

> JOANNA
> He should have been flattered you mistook
> him for a waiter. In my book, waiters are a
> much better class of people than lawyers.

> KATE
> The client was the one who was angry. He
> was quite nice about it.

> JOANNA
> Did he look like a waiter?

                         KATE
          Kind of... no... I don't know. What does a
          waiter look like? He was quite good-looking
          actually. Very... very smooth.

                         JOANNA
          All the top lawyers are smooth. It comes
          with the territory.

                         KATE
          He had a kind of... kind of... he looked a
          bit like Jeremmy Irons. An older Jeremy
          Irons.

                         JOANNA
          Jeremy Irons is old.

                         KATE
          Older than that.

                         JOANNA
          Wow! That is old. Rich?

                         KATE
          I didn't ask. Why?

                         JOANNA
          Maybe he'll loan you the ten grand.

                         KATE
          He offered to help with the dishes.

                         JOANNA
          He what... !

INT. BOARD ROOM KITCHEN -- DAY - CLOSE KATE

                         KATE
          You what!!!

PULL BACK to see Edward.

                         EDWARD
          You wash. I'll dry.

                         KATE
          Listen... I really am sorry... sir... about
          mistaking you for the waiter.

                    EDWARD
          I did once... wait. When I was at law
          school. Needed the money.

                    KATE
          I'm sure you were very good at it. Now, if
          you'll excuse me...

                    EDWARD
          I was terrible, I lasted a week. But I was
          good at dishes.

                    KATE
          I can manage, honestly... sir.

                    EDWARD
          Please don't call me sir. It makes me feel
          even older than I am. Call me Edward.
          Edward Barton-Smith.

He sticks out his hand. A moment and then Kate wipes her own
hands on her apron and returns the handshake.

                    JOANNA
               (voice-over)
          And did he?

INT. OFFICE -- DAY

Back to the two girls.

                    KATE
          Did he what?

                    JOANNA
          Help with the dishes.

                    KATE
          No... of course not. But he took our card.
          Said he's like us to cater a dinner party
          at his home.

Joanna takes the card and glances at it.

                    JOANNA
          Edward Barton Smith QC, Lincoln's Inn
          Field. What kind of an address is that! It
          sounds like he works down on the farm.

                    KATE
It's where all the top lawyers have their
offices.

                    JOANNA
In a field!

                    KATE
It's here in London. Part of the law courts.

                    JOANNA
So why don't they call it Lincolns Inn
Road... or Boulevard. Fields... God, that's
so English.
    (thinks a moment)
QC. Of course! They wear those cute little
wigs. Why do they do that?

                    KATE
It's just another boring English tradition,
I suppose. Like... I don't know... like...

                    JOANNA
Like the Royal family. They're a boring
English tradition.

                    KATE
You're not supposed to say that. You're a
foreigner.

                    JOANNA
I'm American.

                    KATE
They don't come any foreigner than that.

                    JOANNA
Was he wearing his wig at lunch?

                    KATE
They only wear them in court.

                    JOANNA
I don't know how they expect the jury to
take them seriously, dressed like that. I
go to law I want an attorney who looks like
an attorney...

                    KATE
Like Ally Mcthingy.

                    JOANNA
          Like Perry Mason. And as for your judges...

She teases imaginary long hair.

                    JOANNA
          I mean... pease... call me madam.

The phone rings. Joanna picks it up. She answers in her best
telephone voice.

                    JOANNA
          Kate's Pantry. How can I help you?
               (ordinary voice)
          No, this is not she... her. Who's calling?
          Oh... sure... hang on a sec.

She holds her hand over the mouthpiece.

                    JOANNA
          It's Mister QC.

Kate takes the phone.

                    KATE
          Kate Norman. Yes, of course I remember. It
          was only a couple of hours ago.
               (pause)
          Yes, I think so. Let me look in my book.
          Hold on.

She cups the mouthpiece.

                    KATE
               (to Joanna)
          He wants us to do a dinner party.

                    JOANNA
          He wants you to so a dinner party.

Kate looks at her a beat, then back to the phone.

                    KATE
          Either my partner or I would be happy to do
          that Mr QC... Mister Barton Smith... sorry
          ... Edward.
               (pause)
          Yes... I see... yes. I understand. Very well
          then, I'll take down the details. Just hang
          on a second while I get a pencil and paper.

                          KATE (CONT'D)
                    (cups the phone)
               You're right. Just me.

                          JOANNA
               It's not your culinary experience he's
               after, girl.

                          KATE
               But he's old.

                          JOANNA
               Darling. They're never too old. You said he
               was cute.

                          KATE
               Yes... but...

                          JOANNA
               Make up your mind, honey. He's not gonna
               hang on all day.

          Pause. Finally Kate makes up her mind. Back to phone.

                          KATE
               I'm sorry to have kept you waiting. How
               many people? I see.

          She looks at Joanna and holds up two fingers.

                          JOANNA
               Surprise, surprise.

                          KATE
                    (back to phone)
               I could fax you some sample menus. Then
               when you've made up your... mind. Yes... I
               see... very well then. Yes, my choice.
               Thank you. Goodbye, sir. Sorry, goodbye
               Edward.

          She hangs up, thoughtful a long moment, then she shrugs.

                          KATE
               Maybe we're barking up the wrong tree. He
               could be entertaining a colleague... a lady
               friend even.

                          JOANNA
               Dream on, girl. When's the big event?

                    KATE
Tuesday... seven thirty.

                    JOANNA
OK. Here's what you do. You come on a bit
strong... sex it up a bit... you know what
I mean. Then, when you've got him
panting... really panting, that's when you
ask him to loan you ten tousand pounds.

                    KATE
You really think he'll make a play for me?

                    JOANNA
Come on, sweetie. Where have you been all
your life!

                    KATE
I've had my share.

                    JOANNA
Tell me about it. I met a couple of them...
remember. The one with the dreadlocks who
didn't wear socks.

                    KATE
David.

                    JOANNA
Then there was the pin-stripe wonder with
greedy hands and a ring round his collar.

                    KATE
    (grin)
They weren't that bad. Yeah, I guess they
were. Unlucky in love, I suppose. What'll I
do if he does make a pass?

                    JOANNA
Shoot! He's a lawyer. Ask for some legal
advice. Anything will do. Tell him you're
thinking of bringing a medical malpractice
case... they love those back home. Soon as
he says anything, you've got him. He tries
anything after that he could be disbarred
for making sexual advances to a client.
That's when you ask him for the ten grand.

Kate starts to fiddle with some dishes or papers, whatever.
Joanna watches her for a beat.

> JOANNA
> Listen. You don't have to do it if you
> don't want to.

CLOSE — KATE

Thinking about it.

IMAGINATION SEQUENCE

These sequences are cut in from time to time. They represent
Kate's idea of what might take place. They should be overlit
and shot with a slightly soft filter. There will be no
dialogue.

INT. DREAM DINING ROOM -- NIGHT

A table in the centre of the room, place settings of fine
cutlery and glass for two. Edward, in a dinner jacket, is
seated at the table. Now he turns as the door to the kitchen
opens and Kate comes in carrying a covered serving platter.
She is wearing a cute, frilly apron over a very smart, sexy
dress. She sweeps towards the table where she deposits the
platter in front of Edward. She removes the cover with a
flourish to disclose a roast suckling pig or a fully dressed
pheasant... something opulent. Then she moves around and
takes her own seat. Edward stands up. He produces from his
pocket a remote control and clicks it towards a hidden
stereo. Immediately romantic music fills the air, a waltz.
He comes around to Kate, bows and indicates that he would like
to dance. She rises into his arms and they whirl around the
room for a couple of turns; then he leads her back to the
table. She sits and he goes to the sideboard, where he picks
up a serving platter similar to the one she has fetched in. He
places it in front of her and removes the cover with a
flourish. On the platter, in neatly tied packets, is ten
thousand pounds.

CLOSE KATE

Looking at the money with delight.

> JOANNA
> (voice-over)
> Did you hear me?

INT. OFFICE -- DAY

Kate and Joanna as Kate pulls herself back together.

> KATE

Mm?

> JOANNA

I said you don't have to do it if you don't
want to.

> KATE

I don't know. I'm quite looking forward to
it.

INT. BARTON SMITH KITCHEN -- NIGHT

The kitchen in Edward's apartment. Kate is busy doing whatever
it is needs doing to get dinner together. Under her apron (a
proper apron) she's wearing the same sexy dress. Now the door
opens and Edward comes in carrying two martinis.

> EDWARD

A martini for the chef.

> KATE

Oh! I should have told you. I never drink
hard liquor. Just wine.

Without batting an eyelid Edward tips the two martinis into the
sink.

> EDWARD

Just what I'm always telling my clients.
Stick to the grapes.

Over to the fridge where he takes out a bottle of champagne.

> KATE

Listen... don't open that just for my sake.
I'm driving.

> EDWARD

Don't worry. My guest likes champagne.

He turns and goes out, leaving a surprised and slightly disap-
pointed Kate.

> KATE

Shoot!

She turns back and starts to rattle some pots and pans. She's
quite a bit put-out. A moment later, Edward sticks his head
back in.

                         EDWARD
          Bad news I'm afraid. My guest just cancelled.

                         KATE
          When?

                         EDWARD
          Just now. On the phone. Didn't you hear the
          phone?

                         KATE
          No... I didn't.

                         EDWARD
          Pity to waste all this food though... how
          about you and I...

Kate smiles.

                         KATE
          What a nice idea.

DISSOLVE

INT. EDWARD'S DINING ROOM -- NIGHT

Dinner is in progress. They are on their starters.

                         KATE
          It seemed everyone was into parties. Lunch
          parties, dinner parties, supper parties,
          party parties. I like to cook so Joanna and
          I, she's my partner, we pooled our meagre
          resources, borowed some money... lots of
          money... from the bank... and Kate's Pantry
          was launched.

                         EDWARD
          Successfully, I trust.

                         KATE
          Oh! The launch was a wow. Then things
          slowed down a bit. In fact, if I don't come
          up with... no, it's boring.

                         EDWARD
          So bore me.

                         KATE
          Bank managers. God preserve me from bank

managers... your friendly neighborhood
highwaymen.

                    EDWARD
          Overdraft?

                    KATE
          More like a gale than a draft. Still, we
          don't want to talk about that. Like I
          said... it's boring. More starters... ?

                    EDWARD
          There's more?

                    KATE
          I cater for healthy appetites.

                    EDWARD
          In which case...

She starts to clear from the table.

                    EDWARD
          No. Let me. I insist..

He starts into the kitchen. At that moment the doorbell rings.

                    EDWARD
          Get that for me, will you?

INT. BARTON SMITH HALLWAY -- NIGHT

Kate over to the front door. Just before she reaches it it
is opened from the outside by MARY, a smart, attractive, good-
looking 55-year-old woman. She has used her own key and now she
turns and picks up a suitcase she has brought with her and
comes in.

                    MARY
          My goodness... what a heavenly smell of
          cooking.
              (to Kate)
          Don't tell me. You must be Jason's new
          girlfriend.

                    KATE
          Who's Jason?

                    MARY
          My son... our son. Where is Edward, anyway?

                    KATE
          He's in the kitchen.

                    MARY
          Then you must be a friend of Jennifer's.
          Right?

                    KATE
          Jennifer your daughter. The daughter of you
          and Edward.

                    MARY
             (curious)
          Yes?

                    KATE
          And you've just arrived back unexpectedly.
          I mean... like you aren't supposed to be
          here. Not now, that is. I mean, you're
          supposed to be here, but not right now.
          Right?

She's babbling.

                    MARY
          Are you feeling all right, my dear?

Kate pulls herself together.

                    KATE
          Yes. Certainly. Edward... Mr Barton Smith's
          in the kitchen.

                    MARY
          You already told me.

Mary looks at her for a short beat then heads for the kitchen.

                    KATE
          Listen... I'm sorry. Really sorry. I didn't
          know. He didn't tell me.

                    MARY
          I beg you pardon?

                    KATE
          Tell him I'll send for the dishes
          tomorrow... along with the bill. And a
          bloody great bill it's going to be. You can
          tell him that too.

She grabs her coat from the hall stand and exits quickly,
leaving a bemused Mary looking after her.

> KATE
> (voice-over)
> I mean. What a creep. Married. Wife's
> away... so let's have some fun.

INT. OFFICE -- DAY

Next day. Kate and Joanna.

> KATE
> ...God! How could I have been so stupid?

> JOANNA
> Join the club, sweety.

> KATE
> He seemed so... nice... I told him
> practically my entire life story. What a
> prize idiot. You know what makes it worse?
> I'd really started to fancy him.

> JOANNA
> Fact of life, honey. The married ones are
> the most fanciable.

> KATE
> ...even if he was old enough to be my
> father. His wife thought I was the son's
> girlfriend. Oh God!

The phone rings. Joanna picks it up.

> JOANNA
> Kate's Pantry. How can I help you? Why...
> hello! Oh, I don't think so. All right,
> I'll enquire.

Cups phone.

> JOANNA
> Guess who?

Kate grabs for the phone.

> KATE
> Give me that...

Then she releases her hold.

>   KATE
>   No. I don't want to talk to him. There's
>   nothing he could say would be of the
>   slightest interest to me.

>   JOANNA
>   (into phone)
>   I'm sorry, Miss Norman is not available
>   right now.
>   (listens)
>   Yes... right... yes, I'll tell her. Goodbye.

She hangs up and starts to busy herself with something. Kate
watches her for a beat.

>   KATE
>   Well...?

>   JOANNA
>   Well what? I quote. "There's nothing he
>   could say would be of the slightest
>   interest to me."

>   KATE
>   (threatening)
>   Joanna...

>   JOANNA
>   He wants to see you.

Kate shakes her head.

>   KATE
>   Unbelievable. I mean... unbelievable.

>   JOANNA
>   He's not married, by the way.

>   KATE
>   What!

>   JOANNA
>   That's what he just said. Tell her I'm not
>   married and I'd like to see her. He has a
>   proposition he'd like to put to you.

>   KATE
>   I bet he has.

                    JOANNA
          A business proposition, he said.

                    KATE
          Great! Now he's trying to buy me. What does
          he think I am? Some kind of a... a... a...

                    JOANNA
               (helpfully)
          Hooker?

                    KATE
          I mean... what else did he say?

                    JOANNA
          Who needs more?

Kate thinks on it a moment.

                    KATE
          I suppose I could... I mean, it can't do
          any harm... can it?

                    JOANNA
          7937 6997.

Kate reaches for the phone.

                    KATE
          Even if it's just to find out who that
          woman was last night.

INT. PUB NEAR LAW COURTS -- DAY

Edward and Kate. Corner table. Glasses of wine and a
ploughman's lunch.

                    EDWARD
          She's my ex-wife. We've been divorced for
          ten years. She'd just arrived back from a
          trip and she'd come to collect her keys.

                    KATE
          If she's your ex-wife, how come you've got
          her keys?

                    EDWARD
          Somebody used her flat while she was away
          and left the keys with me. She lives in the
          same building.

                    KATE
Your building?

                    EDWARD
A lot of people do. There are 15 flats
altogether.

                    KATE
But... your ex-wife... doesn't it... I
mean... isn't it...

                    EDWARD
We're good friends. She's a bright lady.

                    KATE
So why did you get a divorce?

                    EDWARD
I didn't. She did.

                    KATE
Why?

                    EDWARD
She wanted to graze in pastures new. It
happens.

                    KATE
That's rotten.

                    EDWARD
    (shrugs)
I survived. So... that's why you ran off.
You thought I was a married man.

                    KATE
And I thought you were planning to seduce
me.

                    EDWARD
I was.

Slight pause.

                    KATE
She said you've got children... sounded
like they're as old as me.

                    EDWARD
How old are you?

                    KATE
     I'll be 30... soon.

                    EDWARD
     Jason is 29. Jennifer is 27.

                    KATE
     It's not very sensible, is it?

                    EDWARD
     What isn't?

                    KATE
     You and me.

                    EDWARD
     Is that why you agreed to have lunch with
     me? So you could tell me that?

                    KATE
     Yes... I suppose...

                    EDWARD
     I'm fighting a lost cause?

                    KATE
     Yep!

                    EDWARD
     No chance?

                    KATE
     I don't think so.

                    EDWARD
     Very well. I suppose I have no alternative
     but to accept your decision.

                    KATE
     Some lawyer you are. Aren't you even going
     to present a case?

INT. OFFICE -- DAY

Kate and Joanna.

                    JOANNA
     Did he?

                    KATE
We're going to discuss it over dinner
tonight. At least we are if you'll do the
Annan dinner party for me. Everything's
ready.

                    JOANNA
I don't know, sweetie. I had this kinda...
date...

                    KATE
Who?

                    JOANNA
Charles.

                    KATE
You told me you were through with him...
    (afterthought)
...three times.

                    JOANNA
Yeah... well... we all make mistakes...
    (pointedly)
...don't we?

                    KATE
Take him along. He can help you with the
dishes.

                    JOANNA
Sure. If we can afford the breakages.
Incidentally... what was the business
proposition? I mean, that's the main reason
you agreed to see him... wasn't it?

                    KATE:
I forgot to ask.

                    JOANNA
You're smitten, girl. Be careful, he's old
enough to be your...

                    KATE
    (cutting in)
I don't want to hear it.

                    JOANNA
You might as well get used to it. If this
thing goes anyplace, you're going to be

hearing it a lot. Where's he taking you to
dinner? Or is he having it catered?

            KATE
Out. Somewhere intimate.

            JOANNA
Is that what he said?

            KATE
No. That's what I'm hoping.

            JOANNA
And afterwards? Back to his place?

            KATE
Good heavens, no! On our first date? What
kind of girl do you take me for!

            JOANNA
You're frightened the ex-wife might put in
another appearance. Right?

            KATE
Right!

            JOANNA
Well, you can't bring him back here.

            KATE
Why not?

            JOANNA
Because I live here too. Remember our
number one house rule. No sleep over
guests.

            KATE
Couldn't you stay at Charlie's? Just this
once?

            JOANNA
Charlie doesn't have a place any more. I
think that's why we've got this date. He's
gonna try talking me into letting him move
in here.

            KATE
OK! So I don't bring Edward back here.

                    JOANNA
Which doesn't matter because you just said
you wouldn't go to bed with him on your
first date anyway.

                    KATE
Yeah, well I only said that 'cause I... you
know...

                    JOANNA
You're a properly brought-up young lady and
you feel duty-bound to say it.

                    KATE
Right.

                    JOANNA
In fact it's your third date. You've already
cooked him dinner and had a pub lunch.

                    KATE
And she's not likely to put in another
appearance... the ex-wife. And even if she
does... like she needs to borrow a cup of
sugar... I mean... she's been ex for ten
years. And she was the one to leave him so
she was obviously playing around at the
time. In any event...

                    JOANNA
Keep talking, girl. A couple more minutes
and you'll have convinced yourself it's OK
to go back to his place.

                    KATE
Always providing he asks me.

                    JOANNA
He'll ask. And when he does I wish you
luck, girl. You deserve it. And don't
forget, business before pleasure. Find out
what the business proposition is before you
succumb.
                    KATE
It doesn't seem... right, somehow. Like I'm
selling myself.

                    JOANNA
So if it'll make you feel any better, go to
bed with him first. But don't let

post-coital euphoria blind you to the main
issue.

>   KATE
What a heavenly thought.

>   JOANNA
What?

>   KATE
Post-coital euphoria. The last affair I had
I was supposed to feel post-coital grati-
tude ...like he'd done me a big favour.

>   JOANNA
How do they manage that? Charles makes me
feel I should get up and cook him something
to eat.

>   KATE
I think Edward will be different.

>   JOANNA
Why should he?

>   KATE
He's got beautiful manners.

>   JOANNA
So maybe he'll say thank you before he
rolls over and starts snoring.

>   KATE
I don't think so. No... it's going to be
different... I know it is.

IMAGINATION SEQUENCE

A bedroom. Edward, in an elegant robe, is leading a slightly
nervous Kate towards a huge, overdraped fourposter. She is
wearing something diaphanous which manages to float a lot
around the edges. He seats her on the bed, then he reaches into
a bedside drawer and produces a remote control, which
he uses to switch on the magical music that he did in the last
dream sequence. He turns back to her and gently pushes her
backwards as he embraces her, kissing her deeply,
passionately. A sudden CRASH of sound and they both turn. There
at the bedroom door stands Mary. She is furious, distraught,
wild-eyed... you name it... and in her hand she has a very
large revolver. Now she raises it, aiming it at the lovers.

>   JOANNA
>   (voice-over)
>   I hope you're right... I really do.

INT. OFFICE -- DAY

Kate and Joanna. Now Kate pulls herself together.

>   KATE
>   Maybe it's not such a good idea after all.

>   JOANNA
>   Don't worry about it. He might not even ask
>   you.

INT. BARTON SMITH HALLWAY -- NIGHT

Outside the front door. Kate and Edward. They've had their
dinner and, as Edward unlocks the door, she is looking around
the hallway at the other front doors.

>   KATE
>   Which is your wife's apartment?

>   EDWARD
>   Ex-wife.

>   KATE
>   Whatever. Which is hers?

>   EDWARD
>   It's on the top floor. The penthouse. Very
>   grand. The best in the whole building.

He opens the door and they go in.

ANGLE INSIDE APARTMENT

Edward takes her coat.

>   EDWARD
>   Here. Let me...

>   KATE
>   How come she's got the grand apartment? I
>   mean... this is very nice but...

>   EDWARD
>   She owns the building... that's how. Now, a
>   glass of champagne.

>   KATE
>   I don't know, Edward. Is this a good idea?
>   I mean... well... we've only just met...
>   and you're... I'm... For God's sake,
>   convince me!

>   EDWARD
>   There's only one way I can think of to do
>   that.

He takes her by the hand and leads her towards the bedroom
door. Kate is very nervous suddenly.

>   KATE
>   No... I don't think so.

>   EDWARD
>   Why not?

>   KATE
>   Its not.... right.

>   EDWARD
>   Two adults attracted to each other. No
>   ties. No commitments. Why isn't it right?

>   KATE
>   I'll tell you why it's not right. If I go
>   to bed with you now I'll never know whether
>   it's because I really want to, which I'm
>   pretty sure I do, or because of this bloody
>   business proposition which has been
>   dangling in front of my face like some
>   giant carrot these past few days. Do you
>   understand what I'm getting at?

>   EDWARD
>   I understand perfectly and it's very sweet.
>   We'll discuss business first. Then, after-
>   wards, you can come to bed with a clear
>   conscience. How does that sound?

>   KATE
>   Am I being silly?

>   EDWARD
>   A little. But as I said, I think it's
>   sweet.

He leads across and opens a door.

> EDWARD
> There's some champagne waiting to be opened
> on the sideboard... I won't be a couple of
> minutes.

> KATE
> Where are you going?

> EDWARD
> You said you wanted to hear the proposition.

> KATE
> I do.

> EDWARD
> So... you're a catering expert... open the
> champagne. I'll be right back.

And, turning, he heads off. She goes through, slightly
mystified.

INT. EDWARD'S DINING ROOM -- NIGHT

Kate comes in and over to the sideboard. Sure enough, a bottle
of champagne in the ice bucket. She's about to open it when she
changes her mind. She moves to the mirror over the fireplace to
check her hair and make-up. Her mirror image starts to speak to
her.

> MIRROR IMAGE
> What are you doing, Kate Norman? Joanna's
> right. He's old enough to be your father.

> KATE
> Yours too.

> MIRROR IMAGE
> I mean... what will mummy and daddy say if
> they ever get to meet him? What will we say
> if we ever get to meet his kids? Kids...
> ha! We could be their slightly older sister
> and here we are about to have sex with
> their father. No, it's not going to work.
> Let's get out of here while we still can.

Kate thinks a moment, then she turns towards the door.

> MIRROR IMAGE
> On the other hand...

Kate turns back.

>   MIRROR IMAGE
>   Maybe we should hang around just a bit longer
>   ... at least find out what he's proposing.

>   KATE
>   Apart from bed.

>   MIRROR IMAGE
>   Exactly.

>   KATE
>   Then we'll go to bed with him... right!

>   MIRROR IMAGE
>   That's my girl!

There is a sound from the door and she turns.

ANGLE - HER POV

Mary is coming towards her, her hair all over the place and in
her hand she's holding a large revolver.

>   MARY
>   There you are...

CLOSE - KATE

Horror-struck, she faints.

INT. OFFICE -- DAY

Kate and Joanna.

>   KATE
>   I pretended to faint.

>   JOANNA
>   Why?

>   KATE
>   I didn't think she'd shoot me if I fainted.

>   JOANNA
>   Shoot you with a hair dryer!!

>   KATE
>   I thought it was a gun.

JOANNA
Why would you... a gun!!

KATE
You wouldn't understand. Anyway, he'd gone
upstairs to get Mary. That's her name,
Mary.

JOANNA
Three in a bed. Kinky!

KATE
No. The business proposition. It was her
idea all along. That night she came home
unexpectedly and I ran out, she stayed and
ate the dinner I'd cooked. Edward told her
all about me and she was so impressed with
my cooking that she was prepared to invest
some money in the business. She's very
rich, incidentally.

JOANNA
So... we've got a third partner.

KATE
Strictly hands off. Doesn't want to know.
Her accountant will deal with all the
figures and we'll give her a 20 per cent
discount every time we cater an affair for
her. Every time you cater an affair for
her.

JOANNA
What about Edward?

KATE
What about him?

JOANNA
Did you... I mean did you hang around
afterwards?

KATE
How could I? It wouldn't have been... I
don't know. I mean, after talking business
with his ex-wife... well.. would it?

JOANNA
So you still haven't.

                    KATE
          Nope!

                    JOANNA
          Are you going to?

                    KATE
          I certainly hope so. He said he'd call. But
          I don't know. He didn't seem too pleased
          when I said good night.

She looks towards the phone wistfully for a moment. Then she
pulls herself together.

                    KATE
          OK. Let's get on with it. What have we got
          on the books for this week?

                    JOANNA
          A ladies' lunch on Wednesday... 12 people.
          Then we're empty until...

                    KATE
          Do you think he'll call?

                    JOANNA
          Search me... I mean... men! Who can figure
          them?

                    KATE
          Anyway. Who cares... there's plenty other
          fish in the sea.

                    JOANNA
          Right!

                    KATE
          Who needs the aggravation!

                    JOANNA
          That's what I say.

                    KATE
          In fact I hope he doesn't call. It'll be
          better all round.

                    JOANNA
          Absolutely.

The phone rings and Kate grabs it before Joanna can.

                    KATE
          Hello... !

Her eyes light up and she smiles broadly.

                    KATE
          Speaking...

FADE OUT

               THE END

That's it. I tried for a combination of *Bridget Jones/Sex in the City/Coupling*, not a very original concept, I'm afraid. But always remember, everybody wants to jump onto everyone else's bandwagon, providing it's a successful one, and as I'm not going to put *Dream Girl* on the market, I took the easy route of letting the characters tell the story. The basic plot-line or pitch would never get off the ground. In fact, it's so insubstantial I don't think I can even put it down.

In the unlikely event the pilot idea went any further, I visualised half a dozen shows where Kate and Edward never got it on. Every time they tried, another obstacle reared its head. First Kate decides that she doesn't want to have sex with Edward for the first time in his apartment, so maybe they plan a ski-ing trip and Edward breaks his leg first day out. They plan to fly to the Caribbean, but the airline is grounded and they spend a couple of days hanging around the airport. Kate tries to bring him back to her place, only to get entangled with Joanna and her current date who turns out to be a guy whom Edward recently prosecuted. Etc.

Basically, what I'm saying is that if you fancy yourself as a sitcom writer, have a go. It's probably the most difficult TV market to break into, but if you *do* make it, the rewards are pretty impressive. Try sending a script to the BBC Comedy Development Unit. They'll acknowledge receipt and somewhere down the line they'll get around to reading it. If the first reader thinks it has promise, he'll pass it on to a second reader. Eventually it will get to the head honcho who may, if you're very lucky, decide to go ahead and work with you on further development. But bear in mind, don't try to do what I've just done, your version of *Friends* or *The Office* or any other successful show for that matter. Come up with something different, original and, hopefully, hilariously funny.

But, until then, back to episodic TV. The thing about writing for established shows is that, while the rules of dramatic construction, dialogue, characterisation remain the same as they do in feature films, the writer is bound by the already well -stablished lead characters and the style of the show. While I was script consultant on *Movin' On*, one writer, who shall be nameless, came up with a storyline where our two guys get involved in some fraças purely because they're fall-down drunk. What I'm saying here is, if your heroes are a couple of truck drivers, you don't have them go out and get drunk. I remember well one of the main instructions I gave to writers I employed on episodic shows: "Go away and write the script, but please don't give me any surprises."

The other TV market is the Movie of the Week. I wrote ten of these in all, starting way back when ABC in America first came up with the idea of making movies especially for TV. The fact my first two turned out to be a disaster for yours truly had nothing to do with the writing, which was a straightforward adaptation of my first two novels *Private I* and *Foreign Exchange*. No problem. You own the rights in the novels and you sell them to ABC who give you a chunk of money from which you pay yourself a fee for writing the scripts. All very cosy and, with ABC operating 6000 miles away, they didn't have much say in how the scripts turned out.

Having said that, I have to admit that, if the scripts had been terrible, they could and probably would have cancelled the project. But what the hell! They bought the novels and the scripts stayed very true to them both. I think I am incapable of writing a novel which won't turn easily into a screenplay, although the six I've written and had published since those first two sit in my bookcase gathering dust. Then there are the two that never saw the light of day, but we won't mention those.

Back to the subject in hand. Writing a movie for TV is virtually the same as writing a theatrical movie, with certain restrictions. The length must be absolutely spot-on: 75 minutes, I seem to recall, for the 90-minute time-slot they were assigned. And, to some extent, one had to watch the budget – no big crowd scenes, stay away from exotic locations. All conditions I was well versed in. The problem lay in the fact that I was producing them as well, shooting back to back. Eight weeks for two movies.

Storywise, one was a sequel to the other, meaning the lead characters were the same in both films. I wrote the scripts, then, as the producer, I cast the two main leads. As a seedy private eye, ex-secret service agent, I managed to get Trevor Howard. As the two-faced head of the secret service I snagged Laurence Olivier. His scenes were all in his office, a matter of four days' work for both movies. What a coup! I couldn't wait to let ABC in America hear the news.

It wasn't quite "Laurence who...?", but nearly.

And, "Trevor Howard... wasn't he in that Brit movie which takes place on a railroad station somewhere... two middle-aged people who never get it off."

Maybe I'm exaggerating a little, but not much. Anyway, they refused to go with my casting and sent me a couple of faded TV personalities for the strictly English roles. I'm not sure why I'm bothering to tell you this except I just like to get it off my chest occasionally.

The other eight MOW's I did were when I was ensconced in America and knew the rules. There's not much point in my running through structure and characterisation on these projects. The same rules apply when you're writing any other form of shooting script. The only difference is that you have to deal with the network either directly or through the producer who is hiring you. And if you think some movie executives are a little flakey, wait until you meet the TV guys.

But basically, depending on the type of show you're working on, writing for TV is no different than writing for the movies.

If you can get your foot in the door, there is a great deal of money to be made in writing for TV. Especially if the show is a successful one which is repeated. That's when the residuals start coming in. So shelve that movie script for a moment and try coming up with something for the box.

Six

Adaptations

I mentioned earlier in this book that you wouldn't be doing any adaptations, the reworking of somebody else's material, published or otherwise. What I meant was that nobody is going to give you a novel or a play and pay you to turn it into a script. But that doesn't mean that you can't or won't find a novel or short story that you think might make a good movie or TV drama which nobody has done before.

So, assuming the book/play/story is not in public domain, first off you need to know who owns the copyright. This is almost bound to be the author. So call the publisher and ask for the name of the writer's representative, be it his agent, his lawyer, or, if he's no longer around, his estate administrator. Contact whoever it is and tell them that you would like to turn the property into a screenplay. If it's a novel by Stephen King or John Grisham, forget it, but if it's a novel by Charlie Farnsbarnes which only sold a couple of dozen copies, tell them you'd like a free option for six months. And if they won't let you have it for free, negotiate a price you can afford. But, and this is extremely important, don't put pen to paper until you've got some kind of an option contract.

The other way to go in adapting is to find something that turns you on which is in public domain. Charles Dickens is in public domain, so is Shakespeare, so is Mary Shelley and Bram Stoker and Tolstoy and Chekov and the Bible. There's a lot of material out there if you're interested. Good stories, good characters and who cares if they've already been done? *Romeo and Juliet* has been rewritten in every dramatic form. Try one for yourself as an exercise. How about combining *Romeo and Juliet* with *Blade Runner*? Desperately in love, Juliet discovers she's a replicant and tries to shut herself down. Romeo, thinking she is dead and unable to stand the loss, commits suicide. Juliet, being the super android replicant that she is, is brought back to life and is now doomed to mourn Romeo for the rest of time or until she can persuade whatever powers that be to shut her down permanently. Sounds so good I might have a go at it myself.

I've done adaptations, a whole bunch of them. Apart from *Frankenstein* and *Dracula* I've adapted four other novels, a four-hour TV series and a play, *The Anniversary*. (If you're interested in which ones they were, check the credit list at the back of the book.) I also adapted the first two novels I wrote as movies of the week for ABC Television in America, *Foreign Exchange* and *Private I*.

Adapting a play is pretty straighforward. A two-hour play adapts quite easily to a 90-minute screenplay. There may be a slight problem in that the play might be a two-act structure which you now have to turn into three, but the main problem is opening it up for the screen while still maintaining the intimacy of the original setting. Task of the day, read a play by Noël Coward or Somerset Maugham then have a try at restructuring it as a movie.

But books, that's a different thing altogether. Here, you have to decide what you're going to cut out, which subplots, which characters, because to adapt a 250-plus page novel into a 120-page screenplay, *something's* got to go. Read the book a couple of times, break it down into scenes, decide on which characters are superfluous to your plot-line, outline the others. Then break it into three acts and start writing.

Let's go back to *Dracula*, which I wrote about in chapter one, dealing with the three-act structure. Here let's talk about what was involved in reducing a novel running to around 500 pages to a screenplay running around 120.

I hesitate to suggest that you read the original novel. You'll just have to accept my word that the construction is, to say the least, complicated. As I said, the whole story is told in the first person by four different people (along with a few others who pop up from time to time), using diaries and letters. The four chief narrators are Jonathan Harker, Mina Murray, Dr Seward and Lucy Westenra. So, problem number one was whose point of view was I going to write the movie from? Who was going to be my driving force, my hero?

Harker, Mina and Lucy were all victims, which left Dr Seward, who brings in Professor Van Helsing to help him out. It is Van Helsing who knows all about vampires, who leads the investigation and who, eventually, defeats Dracula. He is obviously our hero, even though he doesn't turn up until page 150 of the novel. And with him as the hero, doing all the work, I decided we didn't need Dr Seward.

In the novel, Jonathan Harker, who starts off the whole story, arrives at Castle Dracula as an innocent, becomes a victim of Dracula and finally recovers by the end. But he doesn't serve much purpose in the investigation and conquest of Dracula, so I had him arrive at the castle knowing already what Dracula was with the intention of destroying him. I used him to bring in Van Helsing and then killed him off by page 25 of the screenplay. Another character I felt we could do without was the madman Renfield, who assists Dracula in the last third of the novel. So he went too.

I guess all this amounted to pretty radical changes and maybe some devotees of the novel were offended. But without those changes the movie wouldn't have been made. Hammer would have thrown up their hands in horror and complained about the cost and the fact that they just didn't make movies that ran more than 90 minutes in those days. Then they would have either shelved the subject or, more likely, got someone else in to write it as per their requirements.

I know Coppola stuck much closer to the book with his version, except for the opening sequence, but, don't forget, his movie ran for over two hours. Then again, if I had been given two hours would I have stuck closer to the original? Probably not.

There are times when an adaptation can call for a complete change in the lead character. Not often, I admit, but I was involved in such a situation when I adapted *Frankenstein*.

First there were the restrictions laid down by Universal, namely to stay as far away as possible from any of the previous Frankenstein movies. This was because, as soon as the project was announced, Universal started to gnash their teeth and threatened to beat us to death with their legal cudgels. Never mind the the original novel was public domain, they had made a string of movies and God forbid we should infringe their "copyright".

They needn't have bothered waving their big stick at us. I didn't want to remake a Universal movie, I wanted to make my own. And the number one change I wanted to make was to Frankenstein himself, the most interesting character in the book, the motivator of everything that takes place. The monster couldn't help doing monstrous things. He was the true victim of the piece. On the other hand, everything monstrous that Frankenstein did was well thought-out. Done for a reason. A much more interesting character.

So, something to bear in mind, when and if you're doing an adaptation of somebody else's work, is not to be scared of making whatever changes you think it needs. One assumes that the basic plot-line is pretty secure or you'd not be interested in the subject, but what about the characters? Play around with them a little, have them as you, the writer, want them to be. But remember, it is always the main character, be he a hero or villain, who drives the story forward.

Here's a short story I've always liked. The author, Amelia B Edwards, died in 1892 and my publisher assures me her work is in public domain. Read it, then have a try at constructing it as a one-off TV drama. I don't think it will stretch to an hour, but don't worry about the length right now, just do the adaptation. I'll have a go at laying out how I would go about it, and you can see how your version compares with mine. But let me make very clear, this isn't a competition. There are no prizes. My ideas for the adaptation might be completely different to yours, but that doesn't make it better, just different...

THE PHANTOM COACH
by
Amelia B Edwards

T he circumstances I am about to relate to you have truth to recommend them. They happened to myself and my recollection of them is as vivid as if they had taken place only yesterday. Twenty years, however, have gone by since that night. During those twenty years I have told the story to but one other person. I tell it now with a reluctance which I find it difficult to overcome. All I entreat, meanwhile, is that you will abstain from forcing your own conclusions upon me. I want nothing explained away. I desire no arguments. My mind on this subject is quite made up and, having the testimony of my own senses to rely upon, I prefer to abide by it.

Well! It was just twenty years ago and within a day or two of the end of the grouse season. I had been out all day with my gun and had had no sport to speak of. The wind was due east; the month, December; the place, a bleak wide moor in the far north of England. And I had lost my way. It was not a pleasant place in which to lose one's way, with the first feathery flakes of a coming snowstorm just fluttering down upon the heather and the leaden evening closing in all around. I shaded my eyes with my hand and stared anxiously into the gathering darkness, where the purple moorland melted into a range of low hills, some ten or twelve miles distant. Not the faintest smoke-wreath, not the tiniest cultivated patch or fence or sheep-track, met my eyes in any direction. There was nothing for it but to walk on and take my chance of finding what shelter I could, by the way. So I shouldered my gun again and pushed wearily forward; for I had been on foot since an hour after daybreak and had eaten nothing since breakfast.

Meanwhile, the snow began to come down with ominous steadiness and the wind fell. After this, the cold became more intense and the night came rapidly up. As for me, my prospects darkened with the darkening sky and my heart grew heavy as I thought how my young wife was already watching for me through the window of our little inn parlour and thought of all the suffering in store for her throughout this weary night. We had been married four months and, having spent our autumn in the Highlands, were now lodging in a remote little village situated just on the verge of the great English moorlands. We were very much in love and, of course, very happy. This morning, when we parted, she had implored me to return before dusk and I had promised her that I would. What would I not have given to have kept my word!

Even now, weary as I was, I felt that with a supper, an hour's rest, and a guide, I might still get back to her before midnight, if only guide and shelter could be found.

And all this time, the snow fell and the night thickened. I stopped and shouted every now and then, but my shouts seemed only to make the silence deeper. Then a vague sense of uneasiness came upon me and I began to remember stories of travellers who had walked on and on in the falling snow until, wearied out, they were fain to lie down and sleep their lives away. Would it be possible, I asked myself, to keep on thus through all the long dark night? Would there not come a time when my limbs must fail and my resolution give way? When I, too, must sleep the sleep of death. Death! I shuddered. How hard to die just now, when life lay all so bright before me! How hard for my darling whose whole loving heart – but that thought was not to be borne! To banish it, I shouted again, louder and longer, and then listened eagerly. Was my shout answered, or did I only fancy that I heard a far-off cry? I hallooed again and again the echo followed. Then a wavering speck of light came suddenly out of the dark, shifting, disappearing, growing momentarily nearer and brighter. Running towards it at full speed, I found myself, to my great joy, face to face with an old man and a lantern.

"Thank God!" was the exclamation that burst involunarily from my lips.

Blinking and frowning, he lifted his lantern and peered into my face.

"What for?" growled he, sulkily.

"Well – for you. I began to fear I should be lost in the snow."

"Eh, then, folks do get cast away hereabouts fra' time to time, an' what's to hinder you from bein' cast away likewise, if the Lord's so minded?"

"If the Lord is so minded that you and I shall be lost together, friend, we must submit," I replied; "but I don't mean to be lost without you. How far am I now from Dwolding?"

"A gude twenty mile more or less."

"And the nearest village?"

"The nearest village is Wyke, an' that's twelve mile t'other side."

"Where do you live, then?"

"Out yonder," said he, with a vague jerk of the lantern.

"You're going home, I presume?"

"Maybe I am."

"Then I'm going with you."

The old man shook his head and rubbed his nose reflectively with the handle of the lantern.

"It ain't o'no use," growled he. "He 'ont let you in – not he."

"We'll see about that," I replied, briskly. "Who is He?"

"The master."

"Who is the master?"

"That's nowt to you," was the unceremonious reply.

"Well, well; you lead the way and I'll engage that the master shall give me shelter and a supper tonight."

"Eh you can try him!" muttered my reluctant guide; and, still shaking his head, he hobbled, gnome-like, away through the falling snow. A large mass loomed up presently out of the darkness, and a huge dog rushed out, barking furiously.

"Is this the house?" I asked.

"Ay, it's the house. Down, Bey!" And he fumbled in his pocket for the key.

I drew up close behind him, prepared to lose no chance of entrance and saw in the little circle of light shed by the lantern that the door was heavily studded with iron nails, like the door of a prison. In another minute he had turned the key and I had pushed past him into the house.

Once inside, I looked around with curiosity and found myself in a great raftered hall, which served, apparently, a variety of uses. One end was piled to the roof with corn, like a barn. The other was stored with flour-sacks, agricultural implements, casks and all kinds of miscellaneous lumber; while from the beams overhead hung rows of hams, flitches and bunches of dried herbs for winter use. In the centre of the floor stood some huge object gauntly dressed in a dingy wrapping-cloth, and reaching half way to the rafters. Lifting a corner of this cloth I saw, to my surprise, a telescope of very considerable size, mounted on a rude movable platform, with four small wheels. The tube was made of painted wood, bound round with bands of metal rudely fashioned; the speculum, so far as I could estimate its size in the dim light, measured at least fifteen inches in diameter. While I was yet examining the instrument and asking myself whether it was not the work of some self-taught optician, a bell rang sharply.

"That's for you," said my guide, with a malicious grin. "Yonder's his room."

He pointed to a low black door at the opposite side of the hall. I crossed over, rapped somewhat loudly and went in, without waiting for an invitation. A huge, white-haired old man rose from a table covered with books and papers and confronted me sternly.

"Who are you?" said he. "How came you here? What do you want?"

"James Murray, barrister-at-law. On foot across the moor. Meat, drink and sleep."

He bent his bushy eyebrows into a portentous frown.

"Mine is not a house of entertainment," he said, haughtily. "Jacob, how dared you admit this stranger?"

"I didn't admit him," grumbled the old man. "He followed me over the muir and shouldered his way in before me. I'm no match for six foot two."

"And pray, sir, by what right have you forced an entrance into my house?"

"The same by which I should have clung to your boat, if I were drowning. The right of self-preservation."

"Self-preservation?"

"There's an inch of snow on the ground already," I replied, briefly; "and it would be deep enough to cover my body before daybreak."

He strode to the window, pulled aside a heavy black curtain and looked out.

"It is true," he said. "You can stay, if you choose, till morning. Jacob, serve the supper."

With this he waved me to a seat, resumed his own and became at once absorbed in the studies from which I had disturbed him.

I placed my gun in a corner, drew a chair to the hearth and examined my quarters at leisure. Smaller and less incongruous in its arrangements than the hall, this room contained, nevertheless, much to awaken my curiosity. The floor was carpetless. The whitewashed walls were in parts scrawled over with strange diagrams and in others covered with shelves crowded with philosophical instruments, the uses of many of which were unknown to me. On one side of the fireplace, stood a bookcase filled with dingy folios; on the other, a small organ, fantastically decorated with painted carvings of medieval saints and devils. Through the half-opened door of a cupboard at the further end of the room, I saw a long array of geological specimens, surgical preparations, crucibles, retorts, and jars of chemicals; while on the mantelshelf beside me, amid a number of small objects, stood a model of the solar system, a small galvanic battery and a microscope. Every chair had its burden. Every corner was heaped high with books. The very floor was littered over with maps, casts, papers, tracings and learned lumber of all conceivable kinds.

I stared about me with an amazement increased by every fresh object upon which my eyes chanced to rest. So strange a room I had never seen; yet seemed it stranger still, to find such a room in a lone farmhouse amid those wild and solitary moors! Over and over again, I looked from my host to his surroundings and from his surroundings back to my host, asking myself who and what he could be? His head was singularly fine; but it was more the head of a poet than of a philosopher. Broad in the temples, prominent over the eyes and clothed with a rough profusion of perfectly white hair, it had all the ideality and much of the ruggedness that characterises the head of Ludwig van Beethoven. There were the same deep lines about the mouth and the same stern furrows in the brow. There was the same concentration of expression. While I was yet observing him, the door opened and Jacob brought in the supper. His master then closed his book, rose and with more courtesy of manner than he had yet shown, invited me to the table.

A dish of ham and eggs, a loaf of brown bread and a bottle of admirable sherry, were placed before me.

"I have but the homeliest farmhouse fare to offer you, sir," said my entertainer. "Your appetite, I trust, will make up for the deficiencies of our larder."

I had already fallen upon the viands and now protested, with the enthusiasm of a starving sportsman, that I had never eaten anything so delicious.

He bowed stiffly and sat down to his own supper, which consisted, primitively, of a jug of milk and a basin of porridge. We ate in silence and, when we had done, Jacob removed the tray. I then drew my chair back to the fireside. My host, somewhat to my surprise, did the same and, turning abruptly towards me, said: "Sir, I have lived here in strict retirement for three-and-twenty years. During that time, I have not seen as many strange faces and I have not read a single newspaper. You are the first stranger who has crossed my threshold for more than four years. Will you favour me with a few words of information respecting that outer world from which I have parted company so long?"

"Pray interrogate me," I replied. "I am heartily at your service."

He bent his head in acknowledgment; leaned forward, with his elbows resting on his knees and his chin supported in the palms of his hands; stared fixedly into the fire; and proceeded to question me.

His enquiries related chiefly to scientific matters, with the later progress of which, as applied to the practical purposes of life, he was almost wholly unacquainted. No student of science myself, I replied as well as my slight information permitted; but the task was far from easy and I was much relieved when, passing from interrogation to discussion, he began pouring forth his own conclusions upon the facts which I had been attempting to place before him. He talked and I listened spellbound. He talked till I believed he almost forgot my presence and only thought aloud. I had never heard anything like it then; I have never heard anything like it since. Familiar with all systems of all philosophies, subtle in analysis, bold in generalisation, he poured forth his thoughts in an uninterrupted stream and, still leaning forward in the same moody attitude with his eyes fixed upon the fire, wandered from topic to topic, from speculation to speculation, like an inspired dreamer. From practical science to mental philosophy; from electricity in the wire to electricity in the nerve; from Watts to Mesmer, from Mesmer to Reichenbach, from Reichenbach to Swedenborg, Spinoza, Condillac, Descartes, Berkeley, Aristotle, Plato, and the Magi and mystics of the East, were transitions which, however bewildering in their variety and scope, seemed easy and harmonious upon his lips as sequences to music. By and by – I forget now by what link of conjecture or illustration – he passed on to that field which lies beyond the boundary line of even conjectural philosophy and reaches no man knows whither. He spoke of the soul and its aspirations; of the spirit and its powers; of second sight; of prophecy; of those phenomena which, under the names of ghosts, spectres and supernatural appearances, have been denied by the sceptics and attested by the credulous, of all ages.

"The world," he said, "grows hourly more and more sceptical of all that lies beyond its own narrow radius; and our men of science foster the fatal tendency. They condemn as fable all that resists experiment. They reject as false all that cannot be brought to the test of the laboratory or the dissecting-room. Against what superstition have they waged so long and obstinate a war, as against the belief in apparitions? And yet what superstition has maintained its hold upon the minds of men so long and so firmly? Show me any fact in physics, in history, in archaeology, which is supported by testimony so wide and so various. Attested by all races of men, in all ages and in all climates, by the soberest sages of antiquity, by the rudest savage of today, by the Christian, the Pagan, the Pantheist, the Materialist, this phenomenon is treated as a nursery tale by the philosophers of our century. Circumstantial evidence weighs with them as a feather in the balance. The comparison of causes with effects, however valuable in physical science, is put aside as worthless and unreliable. The evidence of competent witnesses, however conclusive in a court of justice, counts for nothing. He who pauses before he pronounces, is condemned as a trifler. He who believes, is a dreamer or a fool."

He spoke with bitterness and, having said thus, relapsed for some minutes into silence. Presently he raised his head from his hands and added, with an altered voice and manner: "I, sir, paused, investigated, believed, and was not ashamed to state my convictions to the world. I, too, was branded as a visionary, held up to ridicule by my contemporaries, and hooted from that field of science in which I had laboured with honour during all the best years of my life. These things happened just three-and-twenty years ago. Since then, I have lived as you see me living now and the world has forgotten me, as I have forgotten the world. You have my history."

"It is a very sad one," I murmured, scarcely knowing what to answer.

"It is a very common one," he replied. "I have only suffered for the truth, as many a better and wiser man has suffered before me."

He rose, as if desirous of ending the conversation, and went over to the window.

"It has ceased snowing," he observed, as he dropped the curtain, and came back to the fireside.

"Ceased!" I exclaimed, starting eagerly to my feet. "Oh, if it were only possible – but no! it is hopeless. Even if I could find my way across the moor, I could not walk twenty miles tonight."

"Walk twenty miles tonight!" repeated my host. "What are you thinking of?"

"Of my wife," I replied, impatiently. "Of my young wife, who does not know that I have lost my way and who is at this moment breaking her heart with suspense and terror."

"Where is she?"

"At Dwolding, twenty miles away."

"At Dwolding," he echoed thoughtfully. "Yes, the distance, it is true, is twenty miles; but – are you so very anxious to save the next six or eight hours?"

"So very, very anxious, that I would give ten guineas at this moment for a guide and a horse."

"Your wish can be gratified at a less costly rate," said he, smiling. "The night mail from the north, which changes horses at Dwolding, passes within five miles of this spot and will be due at a certain crossroad in about an hour and a quarter. If Jacob were to go with you across the moor and put you into the old coach-road, you could find your way, I suppose, to where it joins the new one?"

"Easily – gladly."

He smiled again, rang the bell, gave the old servant his directions and, taking a bottle of whisky and a wineglass from the cupboard in which he kept his chemicals, said; "The snow lies deep and it will be difficult walking tonight on the moor. A glass of usquebaugh before you start?"

I would have declined the spirit, but he pressed it on me and I drank it. It went down my throat like liquid flame and almost took my breath away.

"It is strong," he said; "but it will help keep out the cold. And now you have no moments to spare. Good-night!"

I thanked him for his hospitality and would have shaken hands but that he had turned away before I could finish my sentence. In another minute I had traversed the hall, Jacob had locked the outer door behind me and we were out on the wide white moor.

Although the wind had fallen, it was still bitterly cold. Not a star glimmered in the black vault overhead. Not a sound, save the rapid crunching of the snow beneath our feet, disturbed the heavy stillness of the night. Jacob, not too well pleased with his mission, shambled on before in sullen silence, his lantern in his hand and his shadow at his feet. I followed, with my gun over my shoulder, as little inclined for conversation as himself. My thoughts were full of my late host. His voice yet rang in my ears. His eloquence yet held my imagination captive. I remember to this day, with surprise, how my over-excited brain retained whole sentences and parts of sentences, troops of brilliant images and fragments of splendid reasoning, in the very words in which he had uttered them. Musing thus over what I had heard, and striving to recall a lost link here and there, I strode on at the heels of my guide, absorbed and unobservant.

Presently – at the end, as it seemed to me, of only a few minutes – he came to a sudden halt and said: "Yon's your road. Keep the stone fence to your right hand and you can't fail of the way."

"This, then, is the old coach-road?"

"Ay, 'tis the old coach road."

"And how far do I go, before I reach the crossroads?"

"Nigh upon three mile."

I pulled out my purse, and he became more communicative.

"The road's a fair road enough," said he, "for foot passengers; but 'twas over steep and narrow for the northern traffic. You'll mind where the parapet's broken away, close again the signpost. It's never been mended since the accident."

"What accident?"

"Eh, the night mail pitched right over into the valley below – a gude fifty feet an' more – just at the worst bit o' road in the whole county."

"Horrible! Were many lives lost?"

"All. Four were found dead and t'other two died next morning."

"How long is it since this happened?"

"Just nine year."

"Near the signpost, you say? I will bear it in mind. Good-night."

"Gude night, sir, and thankee." Jacob pocketed his half-crown, made a faint pretence of touching his hat and trudged back by the way he had come.

I watched the light of his lantern till it quite disappeared and then turned to pursue my way alone. This was no longer matter of the slightest difficulty, for, despite the dead darkness overhead, the line of stone fence showed distinctly enough against the pale gleam of the snow. How silent it seemed now, with only my footsteps to listen to; how silent and how solitary! A strange disagreeable sense of loneliness stole over me. I walked faster. I hummed a fragment of a tune. I cast up enormous sums in my head and accumulated them at compound interest. I did my best, in short, to forget the startling speculations to which I had but just been listening and, to some extent, I succeeded.

Meanwhile the night air seemed to become colder and colder and though I walked fast I found it impossible to keep myself warm. My feet were like ice. I lost sensation in my hands and grasped my gun mechanically. I even breathed with difficulty, as though, instead of traversing a quiet north country highway, I were scaling the uppermost heights of some gigantic Alp. This last symptom became presently so distressing, that I was forced to stop for a few minutes and lean against the stone fence. As I did so, I chanced to look back up the road and there, to my infinite relief, I saw a distant point of light, like the gleam of an approaching lantern. I at first concluded that Jacob had retraced his steps and followed me; but even as the conjecture presented itself, a second light flashed into sight – a light evidently parallel with the first, and approaching at the same rate of motion. It needed no second thought to show me that these must be the carriage-lamps of some private vehicle, though it seemed strange that any private vehicle should take a road professedly disused and dangerous.

There could be no doubt, however, of the fact, for the lamps grew larger and brighter every moment, and I even fancied I could already see the dark outline of the carriage between them. It was coming up very fast, and quite noiselessly, the snow being nearly a foot deep under the wheels.

And now the body of the vehicle became distinctly visible behind the lamps. It looked strangely lofty. A sudden suspicion flashed upon me. Was it possible that I had passed the crossroads in the dark without observing the signpost, and could this be the very coach which I had come to meet? No need to ask myself that question a second time, for here it came round the bend of the road, guard and driver, one outside passenger, and four steaming greys, all wrapped in a soft haze of light, through which the lamps blazed out, like a pair of fiery meteors.

I jumped forward, waved my hat and shouted. The mail came down at full speed, and passed me. For a moment I feared I had not been seen or heard, but it was only for a moment. The coachman pulled up; the guard, muffled to the eyes in capes and comforters, and apparently sound asleep in the rumble, neither answered my hail nor made the slightest effort to dismount; the outside passenger did not even turn his head. I opened the door for myself, and looked in. There were but three travellers inside, so I stepped in, shut the door, slipped into the vacant corner, and congratulated myself on my good fortune.

The atmosphere of the coach seemed, if possible, colder than that of the outer air, and was pervaded by a singularly damp and disagreeable smell. I looked round at my fellow-passengers. They were, all three, men, and all silent. They did not seem to be asleep, but each leaned back in his corner of the vehicle, as if absorbed in his own reflections. I attempted to open a conversation.

"How intensely cold it is tonight," I said, addressing my opposite neighbour.

He lifted his head, and looked at me, but made no reply.

"The winter," I added, "seems to have begun in earnest."

Although the corner in which he sat was so dim that I could distinguish none of his features very clearly, I saw that his eyes were still turned full upon me. And yet he answered never a word.

At any other time I should have felt, and perhaps expressed, some annoyance, but at the moment I felt too ill to do either. The icy coldness of the night air had struck a chill to my very marrow, and the strange smell inside the coach was affecting me with an intolerable nausea. I shivered from head to foot, and, turning to my left-hand neighbour, asked if he had any objection to an open window?

He neither spoke nor stirred.

I repeated the question somewhat more loudly, but with the same result. Then I lost patience, and let the sash down. As I did so the leather strap broke in my hand, and I observed that the glass was covered with a thick coat of mildew, the accumulation, apparently of years. My attention being thus drawn to the condition of the coach, I examined it more narrowly, and saw by the uncertain light of the outer lamps that it was in the last stage of dilapidation. Every part of it was not only out of repair, but in a condition of decay. The sashes splintered at a touch. The leather fittings were crusted over with mould, and literally rotting from the woodwork. The floor was almost breaking away beneath my feet. The whole machine, in short, was foul with damp, and had evidently been dragged from some outhouse, in which it had been mouldering away for years, to do another day or two of duty on the road.

I turned to the third passenger, whom I had not yet addressed, and hazarded one more remark. "This coach," I said, "is in a deplorable condition. The regular mail, I suppose, is under repair?"

He moved his head slowly, and looked me in the face, without speaking a word. I shall never forget that look while I live. I turned cold at heart under it. I turn cold at heart even now when I recall it. His eyes glowed with a fiery unnatural lustre. His face was livid as the face of a corpse. His bloodless lips were drawn back as if in the agony of death, and showed the gleaming teeth between.

The words that I was about to utter died upon my lips, and a strange horror – a dreadful horror – came upon me. My sight had by this time become used to the gloom of the coach, and I could see with tolerable distinctness. I turned to my opposite neighbour. He, too, was looking at me, with the same startling pallor in his face and the same stony glitter in his eyes. I passed my hand across my brow. I turned to the passenger on the seat beside my own and saw – oh Heaven! How shall I describe what I saw? I saw that he was no living man – that none of them were living men, like myself! A pale phosphorescent light – the light of putrefaction – played upon their awful faces; upon their hair, dank with the dews of the grave; upon their clothes, earth-stained and dropping to pieces; upon their hands, which were as the hands of corpses long buried. Only their eyes, their terrible eyes, were living; and those eyes were all turned menacingly upon me!

A shriek of terror, a wild unintelligible cry for help and mercy, burst from my lips as I flung myself against the door and strove in vain to open it.

In that single instant, brief and vivid as a landscape beheld in the flash of summer lightning, I saw the moon shining down through a rift of stormy cloud – the ghastly signpost rearing its warning finger by the wayside – the broken parapet – the plunging horses – the black gulf below. Then, the coach reeled like a ship at sea. Then, came a mighty crash – a sense of crushing pain – and then, darkness.

It seemed as if years had gone by when I awoke one morning from a deep sleep and found my wife watching by my bedside. I will pass over the scene that ensued and give you, in half a dozen words, the tale she told me with tears of thanksgiving. I had fallen over a precipice, close against the junction of the old coach-road and the new, and had only been saved from certain death by lighting upon a deep snowdrift that had accumulated at the foot of the rock beneath. In this snowdrift I was discovered at daybreak by a couple of shepherds, who carried me to the nearest shelter and brought a surgeon to my aid. The surgeon found me in a state of raving delirium, with a broken arm and a compound fracture of the skull. The letters in my pocket-book showed my name and address; my wife was summoned to nurse me; and, thanks to youth and a fine constitution, I came out of danger at last. The place of my fall, I need scarcely say, was precisely that at which a frightful accident had happened to the north mail nine years before.

I never told my wife the fearful events which I have just related to you. I told the surgeon who attended me; but he treated the whole adventure as a mere dream born of the fever in my brain. We discussed the question over and over again, until we found that we could discuss it with temper no longer and then we dropped it. Others may form what conclusions they please – I *know* that twenty years ago I was the fourth inside passenger in that Phantom Coach.

THE END

That's the story Amelia Edwards wrote over a hundred years ago. Read it again. It's better second time round because, already, you should be starting to work out what you're going to do with it to turn it into a one-off TV drama.

As I see it, and, let me emphasise that, what follows is the way Jimmy Sangster reads the situation. There might be a wrong way to go about this, but there is no specific *right* way. And, as far as I'm concerned, the first choice is whether or not we tell the story the same way Amelia Edwards does, namely as a flashback from 20 years on.

The second choice that springs to mind is there isn't much that happens. The last few minutes on the coach about covers it. The long build-up, with Jacob and his erudite master, leads absolutely nowhere. Even if the old guy is an interesting character, he does nothing for the storyline. We need a way to tie him in more, to involve him other than just as a diversion, however interesting that diversion might be.

The first thing I would do is to settle on the period of the story. Although ghost stories fit well into a present-day environment, nowadays the idea of somebody being cut off on a Yorkshire moor, with no means of contacting anybody, is stretching it a bit. Unless... and here we come to the first big decision. After some thought I decided that, for my version, we *are* in the present day, although the story takes place in the past.

Give our hero a name. I'll call him Charles Edwards. Who he is, what he does, has to come out in the first few pages of the script. Is he upper, middle or working class? Is he amenable, arrogant, selfish? Is he rich or poor, married or divorced, with or without a family, a local or a tourist?

We open with a couple of grouse flying across the screen... bang, bang... they hit the ground and a few moments later Charles moves in and picks them up and we see, from the way he's dressed, that the setting is present day. He glances at his watch, then pulls out his mobile phone and dials a number. His speaking into the phone will tell us a lot about his social level, while what he says and to whom he says it will establish whatever else we want the audience to know about him. If, for example, we keep the background that Amelia Edwards uses, he will be talking on the phone to his wife, who is at the hotel they are using for their holiday, probably a spa-type hotel, where she can spend the day being pampered while he goes grouse shooting. All that information about the character can be delivered in the couple of speeches he uses here to tell her that he's having a great time, he's just bagged two birds and he's going on for a bit longer and for her not to worry that it's getting late and the weather doesn't look too good, he'll take very good care of himself.

He trudges a bit and we start to get the sense of isolation. Maybe he pulls out a map to check which direction to head in next or, better, he encounters a shepherd who warns him that the weather is closing in, and to go on could be dangerous. The shepherd's warning is interlaced with a deeper sense that maybe the danger is not just in the weather. But, if he insists on going on, then make sure he turns off before he reaches 'the old carriageway' because, if he doesn't, he could be in real trouble. And he'll know 'the old carriageway' because there's a sign marking it.

So he goes on and, sure enough, the weather deteriorates so much that he completely fails to see the sign 'old carriageway' which maybe has blown over in the wind or is covered with snow or, if we decide not to have snow, has nearly rotted away from age and neglect. In any event, he's in trouble now and he's lost.

Maybe around here, he stumbles and twists his ankle or somesuch, something to handicap him slightly, to make everything more difficult, and he realises he might be in real trouble. He tries to make another phone call to his wife, but she's in the sauna or hot tub or having a massage, and he doesn't get through. So he goes on.

After a time, he bumps into Jacob, as in the story, and follows him home to the house. The house itself is furnished the way Amelia Edwards describes it. And we meet the old man who, for want of a name, I'll call Isaac. Similar situation, except, when Isaac starts starts talking, it's about otherworldly subjects from the start ... ghosts and things that go bump in the night. Charles tries to get a word in edgeways, without much luck, so he just listens. Sometime during this, he tries to use his phone again. This time it doesn't work at all. Looks like the batteries are dead. Isaac wants to know what Charles is fiddling with and, when Charles tells him, he scoffs at the fact that Charles is sceptical about what Isaac has been talking about and yet he expects Isaac to believe the rubbish (ie, mobile phone technology) that Charles is propounding.

Finally, pissed off, Charles comes up with the statement that he doesn't believe in the supernatural, it's a load of rubbish and only idiots go along with it. This shuts Isaac up for a moment and then the old man suggests that, as the weather has improved, perhaps Charles would like to leave now. Jacob will guide him to the crossroads where he will no doubt be able to pick up the local transport which, while a trifle primitive, is quite reliable. Charles assumes he is referring to an old bus or something. And he and Jacob set off, as in the story. And, as in the story, Jacob tells him about the dreadful accident that happened and then he leaves him and heads back home.

As in the book, Charles staggers along the road and now he sees the approaching lights. At the same time *we* see the 'old carriageway' signpost, the one we saw buried in snow/mud earlier. Now it is in pristine condition and in place.

The lights turn out to be those of a coach which stops for Charles. As he gets in we get the momentary impression that one of the outriders is Jacob. And inside the coach, the last passenger we identify is Isaac, dead and putre-fying like the others. Charles throws himself out of the carriage just before it goes over the edge. He doesn't lose consciousness, but breaks a leg or some-such. One more try on the phone and, this time, it works perfectly. He summons help before passing out. Next thing, ambulance. As it drives off, it goes past the drive that led to Isaac's house. Looking out of the window, Charles can see there is nothing there except a very old burned-out ruin. He's told that it was owned by and lived in by a man and his servant who were killed in a tragic coach crash over a hundred years ago.

That's more or less how I would treat this story if I was asked. How about you? Just remember that nothing is sacred, even when it comes to Shakespeare. Think of *West Side Story* among the dozen or so other adapta-tions of *Romeo and Juliet*. And if it's OK to mess with Shakespeare, it's OK to mess with anyone you like. So, if you come across a public domain idea that really turns you on, go with it.

Seven

Any other business

Tension

Providing the audience knows there is something unpleasant/deadly at the end of the corridor, you can have the heroine take as long as you like getting there. The object, of course, is to get the audience onto the edge of their seats. Then the secret is for her to turn the last corner at the end and find nothing, allowing the audience to breath a sigh of relief, before having the villain/monster erupt from beneath the floorboards, whatever, and chop her to pieces. On second thoughts, he can't do that to your heroine, you're going to need her later. So send somebody else down the corridor.

Admittedly, Hitchcock went ahead and killed off his heroine in *Psycho*. Also, Hitchcock said that as long as the audience knows there's a bomb under the table you can play the scene as long as you want. The bomb doesn't necessarily have to be under the table either. One of the great 'tension' movies was Clouzot's *The Wages of Fear*, where the audience spent most of the movie waiting for the explosives in the back of a truck to blow up which, eventually, they did.

But don't milk the situation too much. It's possible to go over the top, especially if you have more than a couple of sequences like this. Come the third time, metaphorically, and when the girl starts down the corridor, the audience won't even care any more.

Breathing space

Try to give your audience a break now and then. If you've screwed up real tension in a sequence, leading to the climactic payoff, give the viewer a moment to relax before you hit him again. I tried it in the second script I wrote, it worked like a dream, so it became a fixture in all my subsequent work.

As I remember, it went something like this:

INT. HALL. CASTLE FRANKENSTEIN – NIGHT
A scene played between Baron Victor Frankenstein and the maid, Justine.
She is angry that Elizabeth has moved in and reminds Victor that she,
Justine, is pregnant by him and unless he marries her as he promised she'll
tell the authorities about what he is doing in his laboratory. He laughs at
her and tells her she'll need proof.

INT. LABORATORY – NIGHT
Justine comes into the laboratory and pokes around. She's confronted by
the monster, who goes for her. She runs for the door but before she can
reach it, Victor slams and locks it from the other side then stands listening
to the dreadful screams as the monster kills her and, incidentally, his
unborn child.

INT. BREAKFAST ROOM – CASTLE FRANKENSTEIN – DAY
Victor and Elizabeth having breakfast, all very civilized. Long silence, then
the first line from Victor: "Pass the marmalade."

The audience loved it. They'd been gripping their seats, shutting their eyes,
whatever, during the previous scene and now they laughed like they'd just
heard the funniest joke ever. Then they settled back, dipped into the
popcorn and prepared to be wound up again. I worked many times after that
for producer Tony Hinds and he always looked for what came to be known
as the 'pass the marmalade syndrome'.

But having said all that I must add a caution. Don't overdo it. Give your
audience too much breathing space and they'll get bored.

Set out your stall

Try to seize the reader's attention straight off. Because if you don't get that
attention, he/she isn't going to read past page six or seven. It can be a piece
of action or a line of dialogue. Always try to start with a grabber up front,
something to grip the reader. Remember, some of these people read upwards
of three or four scripts a day. While they are constantly on the lookout for
good material, they're not going to waste their time ploughing through
something that doesn't excite their interest from the off.

Also, up front show what genre of movie the reader is about to become
involved in. In other words, make sure he/she know it's a comedy or a

heavyweight drama. Pages one and two of *Fifty Fifty* point to it being a comedy both by the character description and the dialogue.

Make sure your script is well typed, correctly formatted, without messy corrections and properly bound. A lot of people say, "Who cares about the layout? I'll do it my way." My advice is, don't. Do it the way that the reader is used to. It's hard on a reader to pick up his fourth or fifth script of the day, open it to page one, and find the format is different to everything else he's been reading. It puts him off right at the start. If you want the layout to be 100 per cent the way people like it, invest in some screenwriting software. I use MOVIE MAGIC SCREENWRITER 2000. It's quite pricey and learning to use it is almost as hard as writing a script, but once you've got it sussed, it can be a great help. It shows you the format for screenplays, sitcoms, plays and even novels. I used it to write *Fifty Fifty*, so that particular script is laid out exactly as the reader likes it.

Always type your character's name in capitals the first time he/she appears. Don't try to tell the director where to put the camera. If, for instance, a character we'll call JACKSON needs to deliver a particularly powerful line which will almost certainly be shot in close-up by the director, resist the temptation to isolate the shot from the master scene, so:

```
CLOSE - JACKSON

                    JACKSON
        I'm gay... !
```

Instead, keep it in the master. For example:

```
INT. ROOM -- DAY
Everyone turns towards the door as it opens and Jackson comes
in. He stops just inside the door, aware he is the centre of
attraction and makes his big announcement.

                    JACKSON
        I'm gay... !
```

Trust me. He'll get his close-up. And the director won't be pissed off that you've tried to tell him how to cut the sequence.

But having said that, you'll notice that I script cuts all through *Fifty Fifty*. There's a method to my madness, at least there is most of the time. Take page 35 for instance, last couple of lines of the scene in the bar:

```
                    JEFF
        Rental what?
```

```
                    STEVE
          Rental auto.

                    JEFF
          Still need keys.

INT. LIMO -- NIGHT

CLOSE on the face of a uniformed driver, GUS, looking into the
back seat.

                    GUS
          Where to, gentlemen?

ANGLE IN BACK

Jeff and the Steve.
```

... and on with the scene.

In my opinion, the scripted CUT there makes the scene read easier and it almost certainly lays out the way the director will shoot it. Or, if he doesn't, trust me, that's the way the editor will cut it.

This is something I do occasionally in my scripts because, having directed a couple of movies, I *see* the cut as I am writing it and I can't resist putting it in. But I don't recommend it on your first few outings. Apart from the fact that you might get it wrong, it can also piss off a director who's reading your script and who starts to think you're telling him how to direct the picture.

Another fancy trick I use occasionally is the dropping back of the first line of dialogue in a scene to the end of the prior scene. I haven't used it in *Fifty Fifty* because I never felt a need for it. But as an example, look at page 48 which, using the above, could have read:

```
EXT. FREEWAY -- DAY

A VW beetle, Patsy's car, cruising down the freeway, Los
Angeles bound.

                    PATSY
               (voice-over)
          You must remember something he told you, for
          Pete's sake.

ANGLE IN CAR

Patsy driving, Jeff beside her.
```

```
                JEFF
        Lady...

                PATSY
        It's Patricia... you can call me Patsy...
```

... and on with the scene.

I'm assuming you already know about the main scene heading, INT. THIS. NIGHT or EXT. THAT. DAY and, at this stage, that's all you should concern yourself with. If the script is to be submitted to America, use the correct size paper. 8.5 x 11 inches (as opposed to the European A4 size paper). Use 12 point courier type. Include a title page with your name and contact details. Set your left margins at 1.5 inches and start the text at the same distance from the top of the page. And, very important, try to watch the use of words. In America it isn't a pavement, it's a sidewalk; it isn't petrol, it's gas; it isn't a lift, it's an elevator; and so on... ad infinitum.

Don't number your scenes. It's a process that has nothing to do with the writer. All that comes far later when the script is being prepared for production and needs to be broken down for scheduling purposes.

Agents

Let's talk about agents. I've had three or four in my time. In London, in Los Angeles and even one in New York. Love 'em or hate 'em, they are a number one necessity. The vast majority of people in a position to invest in a screenplay won't even read it if it hasn't been submitted by a recognised agent. If this sounds paranoid, perhaps it is a little. But what if some guy submits a script to a studio about a six-headed monster terrorising New Jersey and the studio turns it down, then a couple of years later Tom Cruise does a movie about a four-headed monster terrorising Brooklyn. The guy who wrote the six-header is liable to accuse the company of stealing his material. After all, what's a couple of heads between monsters? So... the power brokers don't read material unless it comes from an agent.

This doesn't mean you're dead in the water. Maybe you bump into a guy at a party who's a director and who, after a couple of drinks, agrees to read your script. Then, if *he* submits it saying he's interested, it might get read.

So, how do you go about getting an agent? One way is to get a toe-hold in the business in some way or other. Doesn't matter much as what. I started as a runner. But once in the system you get to meet people who you wouldn't meet otherwise. Somewhere down the line you're going to make contact with an agent.

The bigger the agency the less chance you have of getting on their books. So, when you first start, forget William Morris or CMA and look for somebody who might be a little hungry. Go to a bookshop and check out *The Writers' and Artists' Yearbook*. They carry lists of agencies. Or drop a line to the WGA in Los Angeles and they'll mail you their current list of agents, or else log on to their website. And having settled on the lucky person or persons, you might try dropping them a line.

Dear Mr/Ms Agent,

I have a screenplay which I would like you to read with the object of representing me for this and any future work.

Maybe you send the agent the completed screenplay and maybe it arrives on the agent's desk on a day when maybe there's not much happening at the office and maybe the agent has time to read it. There's an outside chance. Or maybe the agent gets a secretary to read it and she likes it enough to recommend it to her boss. Or, what is most likely, the agent sends it back to you with a short note saying his/her client list is full.

But keep trying. You *need* an agent. And just wait until you've sold your first script. Every agent in town will be banging on your door begging to represent you.

So where do you go if you *haven't* got an agent? Your first port of call, as it were. One way is to try entering your script into a competition like the Nicholl Fellowship in Screenwriting. It's a competion run from America and is open to anyone who hasn't earned more than $5000 writing for film or television. There are five prizes each year consisting of $30,000 felowships. But, like everything, the competition is fierce. In 2001 they received nearly 5500 entries. There are all kinds of tips given for entering a screenplay, including how to have your script bound, watch out for typos, get the line spacing right, choose the right font. Small stuff, but important, and not only for the Nicholl Fellowship. The ground rules they suggest apply everywhere. If you are at all interested in this approach have a look at them on the internet: www.oscars.org/nicholl/basics.html.

Options

Options. Chances are that somewhere down the line somebody will ask for an option on your script. Maybe, if you're lucky, they might even stick their hand in their pocket for the privilege, although this is by no means guaranteed; at least, not when you are starting out. The line will be: "Give me six months/one year to run with this. I'll get it off the ground for sure."

Giving him the year means that you can't market it anywhere else. He as good as owns it for that period of time. At the end of the year when he hasn't been able to get it off the ground, it reverts back to you and you're back to square one or, in this case, square minus one because the property has been shopped around and lost some of its freshness. Also, you are now in the position of not knowing who's read it.

One experience I had with an option was slightly different inasmuch as I *did* manage to make some money out of it. An independent producer, who shall be nameless, took a one-year option on an original spec script I'd written which I called *Leave It to Harry*. It was a good script, even if I do say so myself, and I didn't much like the idea of giving anyone an option. I mean either buy the property or forget it. But I was busy on other things at the time, so I accepted the option money and got on with my life. Exactly one year later the guy asks for another one-year option for the same amount of money. Again I let him have it. Dissolve now to the end of the second year. The guy wants to take the option again. This time I said no. If he couldn't get the project off the ground in two years, he was obviously flogging a dead horse. I told Mark Lichtman, my agent, to turn him down. Mark, quite legitimately, talked me out of it and I pocketed yet a third option payment.

Then two weeks later Mark calls me again. Seems that a bunch of Italian money men in New York were putting up some money to make a movie. They'd got the script and now they were looking for a director that Mark represented. He told them he'd check it out, but he'd need to read the script first, which was duly delivered. After all that, it doesn't take three guesses to come up with the title of the script that landed on his desk. *Leave It to Harry*.

Seems what had happened was that my guy, the one who had taken the options, needed some ready cash so he sold my script to the Italians, forging my name on a contract assigning him all rights. My agent told him that either he pay me the full contract fee or go to jail. He didn't have the necessary amount of money to buy me out and I finally accepted two thirds of my original fee.

There's an extra sting in the tail here which didn't turn up until a few years later. I was in London at the time and Mark called me from LA. Did I want to send the guy to jail, because he'd just pulled the same scam again. He's telling everybody that it's the first time, terrible error of judgment, slip of memory, all that shit. It just needs me to blow the whistle on the earlier offence. I couldn't be bothered.

So, if anybody wants to take an option on your script, check him out before you sign anything. As a last resort, get in touch with me and I'll tell you whether or not it's the same guy.

Directors

Love 'em or hate 'em, they're destined to be as important a part of your professional life as your computer. They are responsible for presenting your work to the audience in whatever fashion *they* feel is best. You, the writer, the creator of the material, have absolutely no say in what he does with your precious script. I'll give you an example.

The first film that I wrote *and* produced was called *Taste of Fear* (*Scream of Fear* in America). It was my debut as a producer. Great, I thought, at last I'll be able to contribute to the transfer of my work from paper to celluloid. The director I hired was a guy named Seth Holt. He had previously been an editor under contract to Ealing Studios, which, in those days, seemed to turn out nothing but hits. Anyway, first day on the set. Seth is working out how he's going to shoot a scene with the two stars, Susan Strasberg and Anne Todd.

"Maybe we'll change that line there and have you say so and so," he says.

"Better if she says such and such," says I, the writer.

"You don't know what you're talking about," said Seth.

"I wrote the bloody thing," says I.

"Who gives a toss what the writer thinks. Fuck off!" said Seth.

I walked off the set, turned round and came back on.

"I thought I told you to get off my set," said Seth.

"That was the writer," says I. "*I'm* the producer."

"You can fuck off too," said Seth.

I'm only telling you this to show you that, once the movie starts shooting, the director has absolute control. Maybe if he's employing a huge mega-star *à la* Hoffman or Redford, or the producer is Jesus Christ, then he might drop the "fuck off." But, make no mistake, he's in charge.

I must just add that Seth Holt and I got on extremely well. He directed another movie I wrote and produced called *The Nanny* and I tried to get him for a third, but he was busy elsewhere. He died over 30 years ago, in the middle of shooting a movie for Hammer. In my opinion, he was a huge talent.

Another director I worked with as a writer/producer was Freddie Francis, two-time Oscar-winning cameraman and director of three movies of mine. A talented, charming man. If I'd tried to change a line on the set while he was directing, he wouldn't have told me to fuck off, he would have listened to what I had to say, nodding his head in agreement, then wait until I'd left the set before changing the line the way he wanted.

The man who directed most of the movies I wrote, I rarely came in contact with. This was Terry Fisher. I had been his assistant director on a number of films, but when I started writing we didn't see much of each other. As I've said earlier, the writer is the last person anyone wants anywhere near the set once the movie starts shooting. There are exceptions, of course. Robert Altman insisted that Julian Fellowes, the writer of *Gosford Park,* was on set throughout production and, if I read William Goldman correctly, he was often around the sets of the movies he's written.

I accept the fact that the director is entitled to behave like Lord God Sir on the set. Directing a movie is a back-breaking job and unless he's in complete control the whole thing can fall to pieces. But the one thing I don't go along with is the *auteur* theory. This is basically the theory that the director is the person *solely* responsible for what is up on the screen. Forget the actors, the cameraman, the set designer, the composer, forget the writer even. The director's name appears above the title... A Charlie Farnsbarnes Movie... as if nobody else had anything to do with it.

Where was the director when you, the writer, typed FADE IN? The only time you'll get a mention is if the film falls flat on its arse and he, the director, will tell everyone it was a terrible script. Read William Goldman's *Adventures in the Screen Trade*, he's pretty scathing about it too. Even if you have no opinion about the *auteur* theory, read it anyway, it's a great book.

But back to you, the writer and the director. Assuming a script of yours has been optioned by somebody, either with or without a fee (probably without), the guy who took the option, let's call him the producer, will try to get a director attached to the property (also without a fee). It's then that you get to go over your script with the man who's going to shoot it. You discuss this, discuss that, agree, disagree and you do a rewrite. Then, another meeting and probably another rewrite, followed by a couple more.

But hang in there, because this is the only time you are going to have contact with the director, the only time you'll be able to get your ideas across. Once the movie becomes a 'go' project, two things happen, one bad and one good. The bad one is that your script is whipped away from you and you're not allowed to touch it again, ever! The good thing is you'll probably be paid some money round about here.

If the previous few paragraphs seemed to come down hard on the writer/director relationship, there are exceptions that disprove everything I've just written. Take the director Billy Wilder. On every movie he directed, he also shared a screenwriting credit first with, among others, Charles Brackett (*Sunset*

Boulevard, The Lost Weekend) and then with I A L Diamond (*Some Like it Hot, The Apartment, Irma La Douce*). It obviously worked for them.

One last word. I was leafing through an old reference book the other day. *The Time Out Film Guide.* 'The definitive, up-to-the-minute, A-Z directory of 9000 films.' Published by Penguin in 2002. Every movie listed gives the director and the cast. Nowhere, in close to 800 pages, does anybody mention the writer.

The Gothics

I guess I should devote a few short words to what I call the Gothics. They are my main claim to fame. On reflection, my *only* claim. These days I get invited to film festivals dealing with horror and/or science fiction subjects where the guest lists can be quite impressive. The last one I went to was in Sitges, near Barcelona. Also attending were William Friedkin, Roger Corman, Rod Steiger and half a dozen others I can't even remember. This was a competition festival and I sat on the jury. This required me to view around 15 movies ranging from the good to the bad, with plenty of the indifferent in between.

Then there is the other type of festival dealing with 'the Gothics' where my fellow guests are mainly people who were connected with Hammer Films. Usually a bunch of middle-aged ladies who once, long ago, bared their bosoms on the screen. I'm sure more of us would be invited, but we're a bit thin on the ground now.

At these festivals I get asked by fans, most of whom weren't even born when the movies were made, questions like "What was the undercurrent in that scene?" "Was I trying to reach the audience's second emotional level when I had Peter Cushing say so and so?" "Wasn't the final scene ferociously anti-Freudian with an overtone of Nietzsche? Why did you write it that way?"

Because they are loyal, devoted fans who've paid good money to come to the festival, I try to give them an answer they can take home with them, like I wrote it that way because the character build-up shows the man involved is deeply into sado-masochistic masturbation... or something equally unreal.

In fact, the reason I wrote it that way, the reason I wrote anything "that way", was for the wages. That's how I made my living, and if it inspired visions of deep psychological characterisation 50 years on, then I reckon I earned my money.

In other words, there is no deep-seated, suppressed psychological motive in my writing Gothic horror movies. If the first successful movie I'd written had been a comedy, then I would probably have stuck to that genre. In fact, if one counts them up, out of the 40-odd movies I wrote, only six were strictly

Gothic horrors, a couple of *Frankensteins*, three *Draculas* and a *Mummy*. It's frightening to think that any notoriety I have is based on those half-dozen scripts because I'm convinced some of the stuff I wrote later was far better. Those, too, I did for wages. Because, let's face it, whatever you write, be it movies, TV, novels, stage plays, the bottom line is making a living.

You might have a message you want to get across, a theoretical proposition that you feel needs airing, whatever. You might, as most of us do, have a passion just for writing. But, bottom line, you've got to be in it for the money too. If you're not, like you're rich and don't need the extra cash, then you are missing the main driving force that propels most of your fellow writers. Doesn't mean you won't make it though. So keep trying.

Factual shows

Another form of screenwriting which may or may not interest you, but which deserves discussing, are the factual shows. By that I don't necessarily mean documentaries, but segmented TV shows about famous old buildings or the five longest bridges in the world or here lies buried somebody who died 4000 years ago and there's his tooth to prove it. I was involved in such a show based on Ripley's *Believe it or Not*.

A good friend of mine, Ron Lyon, had just got an order for a TV series and would I be interested in writing some of the segments and then taking the main unit out on the road with the star, Jack Palance? I was to direct the segments I'd written and, where necessary, rewrite. I'd never done any documentary-type work before and this sounded like it might be fun, so I checked into the *Believe it or Not* offices in LA and started work.

Each piece was loosely based on fact. I wrote a sequence entitled 'Say goodbye to...', dealing with places or things which were doomed to extinction unless something was done about them. There was Venice, the whole city sinking slowly; there was Leonardo da Vinci's *Last Supper*, buried away in a tiny chapel in the middle of Milan and fading fast. The reason I'm bothering to mention these is to point out the importance of research. I said in my autobiography that if a subject needed research, I'd write about something else. That's OK for fiction, but not for documentary work. Get the facts right because that's what your audience is paying to see.

With the above, the *Believe it or Not* element was merely a tag. We showed aspects of Venice being destroyed by the rising waters, we showed Leonardo's *Last Supper* fading fast and ended the sequence with the line, "...unless something is done about it soon, believe it or not, we can say goodbye to these irreplaceable treasures... !"

But to write these pieces required that I knew what I was talking about, that Venice really was sinking in spite of the work that was already being done and the *Last Supper* was disappearing so fast there was going to be nothing left in ten years. I had to know about high tides in Venice Lagoon, the materials used in the original construction of the foundations of some of the Canal buildings, the type of paint Leonardo might have used and how much touching up had been done over the last 500 years.

So when I started work on the scripts I insisted on having researchers working for me. If you can't afford a researcher, aim to spend some time at the library. Ninety-nine per cent of your audience won't give a damn one way or the other, but there's always one of those experts out there who likes nothing better than being able to pick up a phone to the TV or production company to tell them they don't know what they're talking about. They're also inclined to write letters to newspapers on the same subject so that everybody winds up with egg on their faces. So, let me say it again, if you're writing a 'factual' programme, make sure you get the facts straight...

Radio

While writing for radio can hardly be classified as screenwriting, it is still a form of drama and, as such, deserves a few words. In no way am I knocking or denigrating radio drama. While I'm not particularly a fan of *The Archers*, one cannot avoid the fact that it is extremely well-written. And, let's face it, it's been on the air for over half a century, so they must be doing something right. More important, somebody must be writing it, along with all the other radio drama.

I'm not going to suggest you try writing a version of *The Archers*. I'm assuming that's done by a team, the same way that a lot of US TV is done. It may be possible to get on the team if you know the show backwards, pen a trial episode and send it off on the off chance that it'll be read and they'll invite you along to meet the team.

But enough of *The Archers*, let's talk about one-off type drama of which there are dozens. The BBC reads around 15,000 scripts a year spread between 35/40 producers in London and four or five other regions. And this is just the Beeb, there are also overseas markets in Australia, Canada and South Africa among others. And, providing you don't want to make a lot of money, there's no harm in giving it a try because writing drama, whether for stage or screen or radio, follows a basic set of rules which I've already been over two or three times.

Lesson One: Get the structure right. Lesson Two: Go over the structure again, just to make sure. Whether you're doing a 60- or a 90-minute piece, stick to your three-act structure. Act One, introduce the characters and plot-line and make sure the listener knows the eventual aim of those characters; Act Two, everything goes pear-shaped; Act Three, all obstacles are overcome and everyone lives happily ever after.

Bear in mind that everything in a radio play must be done with dialogue. If it is a plot necessity that it be snowing, then somebody has got to tell us that it is. If a character is confined to a wheelchair, we've got to be told; there are no pictures, only dialogue and sound effects and while the sound effects can be pretty impressive at times, they can't replace the visual impact of, for instance, a ghostly figure materialising at the end of a dark passage. That can only be done by a couple of actors.

```
                    ACTOR ONE
        Oh my God! What's that at the end of the
        passage?
                    ACTOR TWO
        Hell, it's the ghost of the dead whoever.
```

Somehow, that doesn't work for me.

But if radio drama interests you, go buy the book published by Routledge called *Radio Drama*. It's by a guy named Tim Crook. Read it, and if you're *still* interested in radio work, have a go! Apart from anything else, it will hone your plotting and characterisation skills.

Novels

I know this book is supposed to be about writing for the screen, but creative writing is just that, be it screen, stage, radio, short stories or novels. I've told you all I can dredge up about screenwriting and a little about radio. Stage and short stories you can forget as far as this book is concerned. I've written a couple of short stories a hundred years ago which never got published and I've never been anywhere near writing a play. But novels, that's different.

For me, it's the most satisfying form of writing. In movies and TV there are a dozen people between you and your audience. Producers, director, actors, they all want to put their mark on the material. With the novel, nobody messes with your stuff. I know your publisher will assign an editor who may or may not gently suggest a couple of changes, but these will only be carried out if you agree. Your words, ideas, visions, whatever, reach your audience exactly as you want them to.

Another reason I like novel writing is that you set your own deadlines. You can write a thousand words a day or five thousand; you can take four weeks, four months or four years; work two hours a day or twenty-two. In fact, I'm reasonably disciplined, something, I guess, I learned from scriptwriting. When I'm on a project, whatever it might be (including this book), I work set hours every day. I have to admit, the number of hours has grown less as the number of years has grown more. Where I used to put in a good six hours at the typewriter, I now manage three on the computer.

A word about computers. I imagine none of you reading this book has ever worked with anything else. In this day and age, everybody has one. In the old days I would write in longhand using a pencil. I would read what I had written, make my changes and then type it up on one of those old-fashioned machines called a typewriter which, when I started, weren't even electric. Then, further down the line, I'd make some more changes and type it up for the second time. I would read what I had just typed and maybe think this could be changed or that could be better. But the hell with typing it yet again. So the finished material would still have a touch of spontaneity left.

On the computer, stuff gets changed, then changed again, changed once more, copied, cut and pasted, spellchecked, underlined, italicised, left- and right-centred. By the time you get through you wonder whether or not you should give a shared credit to Bill Gates. Needless to say, I love my computer.

Finally

In this book, you've read about formatting. You've read the do's and dont's as I see them. You've been told how the i's should be dotted and the t's crossed.

But I can still hear some of you saying, "Does all that stuff really matter?" You've written a hell of a good story, great characters, strong plot-line, surely that should be enough. After all, the buyer isn't interested in the dots and commas, he's only interested in the finished product. Trouble is, if the dots and commas aren't right, then the chances of him liking the piece are diminished because he won't read it.

And I guess that's it. Doing some of the things I suggest in this book might make your good script great. But not doing them could make the same good script terrible. And just to assure you that I know what I'm talking about, I've printed my credits on the next couple of pages. No point in being successful if you're not willing to boast about it.

So, work hard and, above all, have fun.

```
FADE OUT


        THE END
```

Credits

wrote, produced and directed
THE HORROR OF FRANKENSTEIN (EMI)
FEAR IN THE NIGHT (EMI)

wrote and produced
TASTE OF FEAR (Columbia)
MANIAC (Columbia)
NIGHTMARE (Universal)
THE SAVAGE GUNS (MGM)
HYSTERIA (Universal)
THE NANNY (Fox)
THE ANNIVERSARY (Fox)

directed
LUST FOR A VAMPIRE (EMI)

screenplays
A MAN ON THE BEACH (Exclusive)
X THE UNKNOWN (Exclusive)
THE CURSE OF FRANKENSTEIN (Warner Bros)
THE TROLLENBERG TERROR (Anglo)
BLOOD OF THE VAMPIRE (Anglo)
DRACULA (Universal)
THE REVENGE OF FRANKENSTEIN (Columbia)
THE SNORKEL (Columbia)
INTENT TO KILL (Fox)
JACK THE RIPPER (Anglo)
THE MAN WHO COULD CHEAT DEATH (Paramount)
THE MUMMY (Universal)
THE SIEGE OF SIDNEY STREET (Anglo)
THE CRIMINAL (Anglo)
THE BRIDES OF DRACULA (Universal)
THE HELLFIRE CLUB (Anglo)
THE TERROR OF THE TONGS (Columbia)
THE PIRATES OF BLOOD RIVER (Columbia)
PARANOIAC (Universal)
THE DEVIL-SHIP PIRATES (Columbia)
DRACULA PRINCE OF DARKNESS (Fox)
DEADLIER THAN THE MALE (Rank)
CRESCENDO (Warner Bros)
WHOEVER SLEW AUNTIE ROO? (AIP)
THE LEGACY (Fox)
PHOBIA (Paramount)
THE DEVIL AND MAX DEVLIN (Disney)
FLASHBACK (Lions Gate)

UK TV

wrote
THE BIG WHEEL (Armchair Theatre)
I CAN DESTROY THE SUN (Armchair Theatre)
THE KILLER (four-part serial)
MOTIVE FOR MURDER (four-part serial)

US TV

wrote and produced
SPY KILLER (ABC Movie of the Week)
FOREIGN EXCHANGE (ABC Movie of the Week)

wrote
GOOD AGAINST EVIL (Movie of the Week)
NO PLACE TO HIDE (Movie of the Week)
NORTHBEACH AND RAWHIDE (Movie of the Week)
ONCE UPON A SPY (Movie of the Week)
SCREAM PRETTY PEGGY (Movie of the Week)
TASTE OF EVIL (Movie of the Week)
THE BILLION DOLLAR ADVENTURE (Movie of the Week)
THE TOUGHEST MAN IN THE WORLD (Movie of the Week)

US TV pilots

EBONY IVORY AND JADE (wrote and produced)
MURDER IN MUSIC CITY (wrote and produced)
THE CONCRETE COWBOYS (wrote and produced)
YOUNG DAN'L BOONE (series producer)

story edited and/or scripted
over 100 hours of US TV including...

YOUNG DAN'L BOONE
MOVIN' ON
FOUL PLAY
CANNON
CONCRETE COWBOYS
NASHVILLE 99
GHOST STORY
MOST WANTED
BJ AND THE BEAR
THE MAGICIAN
KOLCHAK – THE NIGHT STALKER
SIX MILLION DOLLAR MAN
SWAT
WONDER WOMAN
IRONSIDE
BANACEK
McCLOUD

Novels

PRIVATE I
FOREIGN EXCHANGE
TOUCHFEATHER
TOUCHFEATHER TOO
YOUR FRIENDLY NEIGHBORHOOD DEATH PEDLAR
SNOWBALL
HIGHBALL
BLACKBALL

Autobiographical

DO YOU WANT IT GOOD OR TUESDAY?
INSIDE HAMMER